SUPREME COURT

WATCH 2011

Highlights of the 2010–2011 Term
Preview of the 2011–2012 Term

DAVID M. O'BRIEN
UNIVERSITY OF VIRGINIA

W • W • NORTON & COMPANY • NEW YORK • LONDON

W. W. Norton & Company has been independent since its founding in 1923, when William Warder Norton and Mary D. Herter Norton first published lectures delivered at the People's Institute, the adult education division of New York City's Cooper Union. The firm soon expanded its program beyond the Institute, publishing books by celebrated academics from America and abroad. By mid-century, the two major pillars of Norton's publishing program—trade books and college texts—were firmly established. In the 1950s, the Norton family transferred control of the company to its employees, and today—with a staff of four hundred and a comparable number of trade, college, and professional titles published each year—W. W. Norton & Company stands as the largest and oldest publishing house owned wholly by its employees.

Composition by Cathy Lombardi.
Manufacturing by Sterling Pierce.
Project Editor: Pam Lawson.
Production Manager: Sean Mintus.

ISBN: 978-0-393-91820-5

W. W. Norton & Company, Inc., 500 Fifth Avenue, New York, NY 10110-0017
www.wwnorton.com

W. W. Norton & Company Ltd., Castle House, 75/76 Wells Street,
London W1T 3QT

1 2 3 4 5 6 7 8 9 0

CONTENTS

PREFACE

Supreme Court Watch 2011 examines the changes and decisions made during the Supreme Court's 2010–2011 terms. In addition to highlighting the major constitutional rulings in excerpts from leading cases, I discuss in section-by-section introductions other important decisions and analyze recent developments in various areas of constitutional law. The important cases that the Court has granted review and will decide in its 2011–2012 term are also previewed. To offer even more information in an efficient format, special boxes titled "The Development of Law" are also included.

The favorable reception of previous editions of the *Watch* has been gratifying, and I hope that this twenty-first edition will further contribute to students' understanding of constitutional law, politics, and history, as well as to their appreciation for how the politics of constitutional interpretation turns on differing interpretations of constitutional politics and the role of the Supreme Court. I am most grateful to Aaron Javsicas and Jake Schindel for doing a terrific and expeditious job in producing this edition.

D.M.O.
June 29, 2011

SUPREME COURT WATCH 2011

VOLUME ONE

2

LAW AND POLITICS IN THE SUPREME COURT: JURISDICTION AND DECISION-MAKING PROCESS

The Supreme Court's October 2010 term opened for the first time in history with three sitting female justices. Justice Elena Kagan was confirmed in the summer to replace Justice John Paul Stevens, who had announced that he would retire at the end of the 2009–2010 term. Little over a year earlier, President Barack Obama named and elevated Second Circuit Court of Appeals Judge Sonia Sotomayor. Justice Sotomayor grew up in the Bronx, the daughter of immigrants from Puerto Rico, and then went to Princeton University and Yale Law School. After spending five years as a prosecutor in Manhattan and then working in private practice, she was appointed in 1992 to the federal district court by Republican President George H. W. Bush, upon the recommendation of Democratic Senator Daniel Patrick Moynihan, and later elevated to the Court of Appeals for the Second Circuit by Democratic President Bill Clinton in 1998. Given that background and the prospect of naming the first Latina to the Court, President Obama banked on a relatively noncontroversial appointment, as he did when then selecting Kagan. Justice Kagan, however, had a very different background as an academic with political experience. Kagan was born on the Upper West Side of Manhattan, New York, in 1960, and received her B.A. from Princeton (1981), an M.Phil. from Oxford University (1983), and her J.D. from Harvard Law School (1986). Subsequently, Kagan clerked for Justice Thurgood Marshall, practiced law for three years, and then taught at the University of Chicago Law School, before serving (1995–1999) in the Clinton administration. Afterward, she taught at Harvard Law School and became dean before Obama appointed her solicitor general in 2009. At age fifty, Kagan became the 112th justice, fourth female (following Justices Sotomayor, Ginsburg, and O'Connor), and the eighth Jewish justice to serve on the Court.

The October 2010 term also marked Chief Justice Roberts's sixth term on the high bench. During his first five terms, the Court had an annual average of 8,547 cases on its docket (ranging from 8,966 to 10,256 cases), and continued the trend of granting oral arguments and plenary consideration to less than one percent of the cases on its docket. The Roberts Court heard on average only 81 cases per term, or less than half of what the Court heard 30 years ago when the entire docket was significantly smaller. As in the past, as indicated in the table below, the Court tended to grant cases in order to reverse the lower courts' rulings and to decide more statutory interpretation cases and those involving jurisdiction, practice, and procedure.

■ INSIDE THE COURT

The Court's Disposition of Appeals in the 2010–2011 Term

	AFFIRMED	REVERSED OR VACATED
First Circuit	1	
Second Circuit	2	3
Third Circuit	3	3
Fourth Circuit	2	2
Fifth Circuit	1	4
Sixth Circuit	1	4
Seventh Circuit	2	4
Eighth Circuit	2	3
Ninth Circuit	6	18
Tenth Circuit		
Eleventh Circuit		2
Federal Circuit	3	3
District of Columbia Circuit		
Other Federal Courts		1
State Courts and Other		10
*Totals:	24	58

*Excludes cases decided on original jurisdiction or dismissed for lack of jurisdiction and remanded.

A | *Jurisdiction and Justiciable Conflicts*

In its 2011–2012 term the Court will decide whether Congress has the authority to dictate how the executive branch issues birth certificates for U.S. citizens born abroad. At issue in *M. B. Z. v. Clinton* (Docket No. 10-699) is the validity of a nine-year-old law (Section 214(d) of Public Law 107-228) in which Congress aimed to acknowledge Jerusalem as the capital of Israel, even though the U.S. government does not recognize it as part of Israel. After State Department officials refused to fill out a report on the foreign birth of a boy—Menachem Binyamin Zivotofsky (M. B. Z.)—born in 2002 in a Jerusalem hospital to show that his birthplace was "Israel," his parents sued, seeking to enforce the 2002 law that directed the State Department to do just that, when asked to do so by the parents. A federal district court judge and the Court of Appeals for the District of Columbia Circuit refused to decide the case and held that the controversy presented a "political question" that the courts had no authority to decide. The boy and his parents then appealed to the Supreme Court, which granted review. In addition to considering whether the case presents a "political question," the Court also asked the parties to address the question of whether the 2002 law unconstitutionally "infringes the President's power to recognize foreign sovereigns." Notably, President George W. Bush made precisely that claim in a presidential signing statement when signing the bill into law in 2002.

The Roberts Court in its 2010–2011 term also reinforced its interest in enforcing threshold rules, such as mootness and ripeness (see Vols. 1 or 2, Ch. 2), and thereby avoiding the questions presented, in *Camreta v. Greene*, 131 S.Ct. 1465 (2011). There, Justice Kagan held that a suit against a social worker and a sheriff who allegedly violated the Fourth Amendment rights of a nine-year-old student by questioning her without a warrant about possible sexual abuse was moot because she was now almost eighteen years old and had moved from California, where the incident occurred, to Florida. Justices Kennedy and Thomas dissented.

In its 2011–2012 term the Court will continue to explore standing doctrines in *First American Financial v. Edwards* (No. 10-708). That case involves whether a buyer of real estate settlement services has standing to sue in federal court under either the Real Estate Settlement Procedures Act of 1974 (RESPA) or Article III of the Constitution. Edwards, a home buyer, sued First American over alleged violations of RESPA. Edwards alleged that First Financial paid millions of dollars to individual title companies and, in exchange, they entered into exclusive referral agreements. The Court of Appeals for the Ninth Circuit affirmed a federal district court denial of First Financial's motion to dismiss due to a lack of standing, because Edwards had not shown a concrete injury because she failed to allege that the charge for title insurance was higher than it would have been without the exclusivity agreement. The Ninth Circuit though, disagreed that the damages provision of RESPA gives rise to a statutory cause of action, regardless of whether an overcharge occurred. But the appellate court determined that Edwards had established an injury sufficient to trigger standing under Article III. The Court granted review in order to resolve a conflict among circuit courts over RESPA.

■ THE DEVELOPMENT OF LAW

Class-Action Suits

The Roberts Court has limited the filing of class-action lawsuits in a number of ways (see also THE DEVELOPMENT OF LAW box in Vols. 1 and 2, Ch. 1). In *AT&T Mobility v. Concepcion*, 131 S.Ct. 1740 (2011), a bare majority held that a California law was preempted by the Federal Arbitration Act (FAA), which governs arbitration agreements in order to "facilitate streamlined proceedings" in resolving individual disputes. Under California's law class-arbitration was permitted, but the majority struck down that law for running afoul of the federal statute. Writing for the majority, Justice Scalia observed that "Requiring the availability of classwide arbitration interferes with fundamental attributes of arbitration and thus creates a scheme inconsistent with the FAA." The Concepcions had signed with AT&T Mobility for a "free" cellphone but were charged $30.22 in fees and sales tax, and in turn sought class-action arbitration of their dispute over the charges. Justices Breyer, Ginsburg, Sotomayor, and Kagan dissented.

A bare majority, however, upheld a class-action suit against California prison officials for violating the Eighth Amendment due to prison overcrowding and the conditions of inmates in *Brown v. Plata*, 131 S.Ct. 1910 (2011) (further discussed below in Vol. 2, Ch. 10).

In a widely watched case involving the largest "class action" suit ever, *Wal-Mart Stores, Inc. v. Dukes*, 131 S.Ct. 2541 (2011), the Court overturned the certification of a nationwide class of some 1.5 million female employees of Wal-Mart, who claimed that the company systematically discriminated against them in violation of the Civil Rights Act of 1964. Writing for the Court, Justice Scalia held that such a class was too large and inconsistent with the Federal Rule of Civil Procedure 23(a). Wal-Mart has some 3,400 stores across the country—each with its own managers—and therefore was entitled to individual determinations of discrimination and employees' eligibility for back pay. In other words, Rule 23(a) requires showing a commonality shared by each member of the class and a single indivisible remedy that provides the same relief to each class member. The Court did not reach the merits of the employees' claim, and individual women may sue over alleged discrimination, though in many instances that may prove too costly. Justice Ginsburg, joined by Justices Breyer, Sotomayor, and Kagan, agreed that the section of Rule 23 that permits class-action requests for injunctions or declaratory judgments does not generally allow claims solely for monetary payments, but otherwise dissented. In their view, the women's lawyers had presented enough evidence "that gender bias suffused Wal-Mart's company culture."

A bare majority of the Roberts Court continued its movement toward further limiting taxpayers' standing (see *Valley Forge Christian College v. Americans United for Separation of Church and State, Inc.*, 454 U.S. 464 (1982), and *Hein v. Freedom from Religion Foundation, Inc.*, 551 U.S. 587 (2007) (both excerpted in Vols. 1 and 2, Ch. 2), and the watershed ruling in *Flast v. Cohen*, 392 U.S. 83 (1968) (excerpted in Vols. 1 and 2, Ch. 2), which had extended taxpayer standing to challenge legislation appropriating funds for religious schools. Sharply limiting *Flast* in writing for the Court, Justice Kennedy drew a bright line between taxpayer challenges to state appropriations for private religious schools and programs that give taxpayers dollar-for-dollar tax credits on their state taxes for contributions to non-profit groups that provide scholarships to private schools, including religious schools. In *Arizona Christian School Tuition Organization v. Winn* (2011) (excerpted below), Justice Kennedy held that while taxpayers under *Flast* had standing to challenge appropriations aiding religious schools under the First Amendment (dis)establishment clause, they did not have standing to challenge tax credit programs that permitted contributions to aid religious schools. He did so on the theory that the subsidy for scholarships was not actually from state tax revenues but from donations of taxpayers who then received tax credits. In a concurring opinion, Justice Scalia, joined by Justice Thomas, would have overturned *Flast*. Justice Kagan filed a dissenting opinion, joined by Justices Ginsburg, Breyer, and Sotomayor.

However, the Court unanimously held that individuals could have standing to challenge the constitutionality of federal laws based on a claim that they violate states' sovereignty under the Tenth Amendment, in *Bond v. United States* (2011) (excerpted below).

Arizona Christian School Tuition Organization v. Winn

131 S.Ct. 1436 (2011)

Since 1999 Arizona has provided tax credits for contributions to school tuition organizations (or STOs). Under the program, taxpayers have the choice of making contributions to secular or religious STOs and receiving tax credits. STOs provide scholarships to students attending private schools, primarily Catholic schools. A group of Arizona taxpayers challenged the STO tax credit as violation of the First Amendment's (dis)establishment clause. After the state supreme court rejected a similar suit, the taxpayers filed suit in federal court. In order to do so they had to demonstrate their standing to sue based on a direct harm of a violation of the (dis)establishment clause, such as a mandatory prayer in public school classes. On remand, the Arizona Christian School Tuition Organization intervened and the district court once again dismissed the suit, but the Court of Appeals for the Ninth Circuit reversed and held that the taxpayers had standing to bring the suit under *Flast v. Cohen* (1968). That decision was appealed and the Supreme Court granted review.

The appellate court's decision was reversed by a bare majority. Justice Kennedy delivered the opinion for the Court and Justice Scalia filed a concurring opinion, joined by Justice Thomas, contending that *Flast* should be overturned. Justice Kagen filed a dissenting opinion, which Justices Ginsburg, Breyer, and Sotomayor joined.

☐ *Justice KENNEDY delivered the opinion of the Court.*

To state a case or controversy under Article III, a plaintiff must establish standing. The minimum constitutional requirements for standing were explained in *Lujan v. Defenders of Wildlife*, 504 U.S. 555 (1992). "First, the plaintiff must have suffered an 'injury in fact'—an invasion of a legally protected interest which is (a) concrete and particularized, and (b) 'actual or imminent, not "conjectural" or "hypothetical."'' Second, there must be a causal connection between the injury and the conduct complained of—the injury has to be 'fairly . . . trace[able] to the challenged action of the defendant, and not . . . th[e] result [of] the independent action of some third party not before the court.' Third, it must be 'likely,' as opposed to merely 'speculative,' that the injury will be 'redressed by a favorable decision.'" In requiring a particular injury, the Court meant "that the injury must affect the plaintiff in a personal and individual way." The question now before the Court is whether respondents, the plaintiffs in the trial court, satisfy the requisite elements of standing.

Respondents suggest that their status as Arizona taxpayers provides them with standing to challenge the STO tax credit. Absent special circumstances, however, standing cannot be based on a plaintiff's mere status as a taxpayer. This Court has rejected the general proposition that an individual who has paid taxes has a "continuing, legally cognizable interest in ensuring that those funds are not used by the Government in a way that violates the Constitution." *Hein v. Freedom From Religion Foundation, Inc.*, 551 U.S. 587 (2007). This precept has been referred to as the rule against taxpayer standing.

The doctrinal basis for the rule was discussed in *Frothingham v. Mellon*, 262 U.S. 447 (1923). There, a taxpayer-plaintiff had alleged that certain federal expenditures were in excess of congressional authority under the Constitution. The plaintiff argued that she had standing to raise her claim because she had an interest in the Government Treasury and because the allegedly unconstitutional expenditure of Government funds would affect her personal tax liability. The Court rejected those arguments. The "effect upon future taxation, of any payment out of funds," was too "remote, fluctuating and uncertain" to give rise to a case or controversy. And the taxpayer-plaintiff's "interest in the moneys of the Treasury," the Court recognized, was necessarily "shared with millions of others." As a consequence, *Frothingham* held that the taxpayer-plaintiff had not presented a "judicial controversy" appropriate for resolution in federal court but rather a "matter of public . . . concern" that could be pursued only through the political process.

In holdings consistent with *Frothingham* and *Doremus* [*v. Board of Education of Hawthorne*, 342 U.S. 429 (1959)], more recent decisions have explained that claims of taxpayer standing rest on unjustifiable economic and political speculation. When a government expends resources or declines to impose a tax, its budget does not necessarily suffer. On the contrary, the purpose of many governmental expenditures and tax benefits is "to spur economic activity, which in turn increases government revenues."

Difficulties persist even if one assumes that an expenditure or tax benefit depletes the government's coffers. To find injury, a court must speculate "that elected officials will increase a taxpayer-plaintiff's tax bill to make up a deficit." And to find redressability, a court must assume that, were the remedy the taxpayers seek to be allowed, "legislators will pass along the supposed increased revenue in the form of tax reductions." It would be "pure speculation" to conclude that an injunction against a government expenditure or tax benefit "would result in any actual tax relief" for a taxpayer-plaintiff.

These well-established principles apply to the present cases. Respondents may be right that Arizona's STO tax credits have an estimated annual value of over $50 million. The education of its young people is, of course, one of the State's principal missions and responsibilities; and the consequent costs will make up a significant portion of the state budget. That, however, is just the beginning of the analysis.

By helping students obtain scholarships to private schools, both religious and secular, the STO program might relieve the burden placed on Arizona's public schools. The result could be an immediate and permanent cost savings for the State. Underscoring the potential financial benefits of the STO program, the average value of an STO scholarship may be far less than the average cost of educating an Arizona public school student. Because it encourages scholarships for attendance at private schools, the STO tax credit may not cause the State to incur any financial loss.

Even assuming the STO tax credit has an adverse effect on Arizona's annual budget, problems would remain. To conclude there is a particular injury in fact would require speculation that Arizona lawmakers react to revenue shortfalls by increasing respondents' tax liability. A finding of causation would depend on the additional determination that any tax increase would be traceable to the STO tax credits, as distinct from other governmental expenditures or other tax benefits. Respondents have not established that an injunction against application of the STO tax credit would prompt Arizona legislators to "pass along the supposed increased revenue in the form of tax reductions." . . .

The primary contention of respondents, of course, is that, despite the general rule that taxpayers lack standing to object to expenditures alleged to be unconstitutional, their suit falls within the exception established by *Flast v. Cohen*. It must be noted at the outset that, as this Court has explained, *Flast's* holding provides a "narrow exception" to "the general rule against taxpayer standing." *Bowen v. Kendrick*, 487 U.S. 589 (1988). . . .

Flast found support for its finding of personal injury in "the history of the Establishment Clause," particularly James Madison's *Memorial and Remonstrance Against Religious Assessments*. . . . Respondents contend that . . . the tax credit is, for *Flast* purposes, best understood as a government expenditure. That is incorrect.

It is easy to see that tax credits and governmental expenditures can have similar economic consequences, at least for beneficiaries whose tax liability is sufficiently large to take full advantage of the credit. Yet tax credits and governmental expenditures do not both implicate individual taxpayers in sectarian activities. A dissenter whose tax dollars are "extracted and spent" knows that he has in some small measure been made to contribute to an establishment in violation of conscience. In that instance the taxpayer's direct and particular connection with the establishment does not depend on economic speculation or political conjecture. The connection would exist even if the conscientious dissenter's tax liability were unaffected or reduced. When the government declines to impose a tax, by contrast, there is no such connection between dissenting taxpayer and alleged establishment. Any financial injury remains speculative. And awarding some citizens a tax credit allows other citizens to retain control over their own funds in accordance with their own consciences.

The distinction between governmental expenditures and tax credits refutes respondents' assertion of standing. When Arizona taxpayers choose to contribute to STOs, they spend their own money, not money the State has collected from respondents or from other taxpayers. [R]espondents and other Arizona taxpayers remain free to pay their own tax bills, without contributing to an STO. Respondents are likewise able to contribute to an STO of their choice, either religious or secular. And respondents also have the option of contributing to other charitable organizations, in which case respondents may become eligible for a tax deduction or a different tax credit. The STO tax credit is not tantamount to a religious tax or to a tithe and does not visit the injury identified in *Flast*. It follows that respondents have neither alleged an injury for standing purposes under general rules nor met the *Flast* exception. Finding standing under these circumstances would be more than the extension of *Flast* "to the limits of its logic." It would be a departure from *Flast*'s stated rationale.

Furthermore, respondents cannot satisfy the requirements of causation and redressability. When the government collects and spends taxpayer money, governmental choices are responsible for the transfer of wealth. In that case a resulting subsidy of religious activity is, for purposes of *Flast*, traceable to the government's expenditures. . . . Here, by contrast, contributions result from the decisions of private taxpayers regarding their own funds. Private citizens create private STOs; STOs choose beneficiary schools; and taxpayers then contribute to STOs. While the State, at the outset, affords the opportunity to create and contribute to an STO, the tax credit system is implemented by private action and with no state intervention. Objecting taxpayers know that their fellow citizens, not the State, decide to contribute and in fact make the contribution. These considerations prevent any injury the objectors may suffer from being fairly traceable to the government. . . .

Furthermore, if a law or practice, including a tax credit, disadvantages a particular religious group or a particular nonreligious group, the disadvantaged party would not have to rely on *Flast* to obtain redress for a resulting injury. Because standing in Establishment Clause cases can be shown in various ways, it is far from clear that any nonbinding *sub silentio* holdings in the cases respondents cite would have depended on *Flast*.

If an establishment of religion is alleged to cause real injury to particular individuals, the federal courts may adjudicate the matter. Like other constitutional provisions, the Establishment Clause acquires substance and meaning when explained, elaborated, and enforced in the context of actual disputes. That reality underlies the case-or-controversy requirement, a requirement that has not been satisfied here.

Few exercises of the judicial power are more likely to undermine public confidence in the neutrality and integrity of the Judiciary than one which casts the Court in the role of a Council of Revision, conferring on itself the power to invalidate laws at the behest of anyone who disagrees with them. In an era of frequent litigation, class actions, sweeping injunctions with prospective effect, and continuing jurisdiction to enforce judicial remedies, courts must be more careful to insist on the formal rules of standing, not less so. Making the Article III standing inquiry all the more necessary are the significant implications of constitutional litigation, which can result in rules of wide applicability that are beyond Congress' power to change. . . .

□ *Justice KAGAN, with whom Justice GINSBURG, Justice BREYER, and Justice SOTOMAYOR join, dissenting.*

For almost half a century, litigants like the Plaintiffs have obtained judicial review of claims that the government has used its taxing and spending power in violation of the Establishment Clause. Beginning in *Flast v. Cohen* and continuing in case after case for over four decades, this Court and others have exercised jurisdiction to decide taxpayer-initiated challenges not materially different from this one. Not every suit has succeeded on the merits, or should have. But every taxpayer-plaintiff has had her day in court to contest the government's financing of religious activity.

Today, the Court breaks from this precedent by refusing to hear taxpayers' claims that the government has unconstitutionally subsidized religion through its tax system. These litigants lack standing, the majority holds, because the funding of religion they challenge comes from a tax credit, rather than an appropriation. A tax credit, the Court asserts, does not injure objecting taxpayers, because it "does not extract and spend [their] funds in service of an establishment."

This novel distinction in standing law between appropriations and tax expenditures has as little basis in principle as it has in our precedent. Cash grants and targeted tax breaks are means of accomplishing the same government objective—to provide financial support to select individuals or organizations. Taxpayers who oppose state aid of religion have equal reason to protest whether that aid flows from the one form of subsidy or the other. Either way, the government has financed the religious activity. And so either way, taxpayers should be able to challenge the subsidy.

Still worse, the Court's arbitrary distinction threatens to eliminate all occasions for a taxpayer to contest the government's monetary support of religion. Precisely because appropriations and tax breaks can achieve identical objectives, the government can easily substitute one for the other. Today's opinion thus enables the government to end-run *Flast*'s guarantee of access to the Judiciary. From now on, the government need follow just one simple rule—subsidize through the tax system—to preclude taxpayer challenges to state funding of religion.

And that result—the effective demise of taxpayer standing—will diminish the Establishment Clause's force and meaning. Sometimes, no one other than taxpayers has suffered the injury necessary to challenge government sponsorship of religion. Today's holding therefore will prevent federal courts from determining whether some subsidies to sectarian organizations comport with our Constitution's guarantee of religious neutrality. Because I believe these challenges warrant consideration on the merits, I respectfully dissent from the Court's decision. . . .

Bond v. United States

131 S.Ct. 2355 (2011)

Carol Anne Bond discovered that her husband had impregnated a close friend and began harassing her. The woman suffered burns after Bond put caustic substances on objects she was likely to touch. Bond was arrested and indicted for violating a federal statute forbidding the "knowing possession or use, for nonpeaceful purposes, of a chemical that can cause death, temporary incapacitation or permanent harm to humans," and which is part of a federal law implementing a treaty ratified by the United States. Bond entered a guilty plea but reserved the right to appeal on the ground that the statute violated the Tenth Amendment and states' sovereignty. After her conviction, the Court of Appeals for the Third Circuit held that she lacked standing to challenge the constitutionality of a federal statute, on which she was convicted, based on the claim that the law violated the Tenth Amendment. Bond appealed and the Court granted review.

The appellate court's decision was reversed in an opinion delivered by Justice Kennedy. Justice Ginsburg filed a concurring opinion.

☐ *Justice KENNEDY delivered the opinion of the Court.*

This case presents the question whether a person indicted for violating a federal statute has standing to challenge its validity on grounds that, by enacting it, Congress exceeded its powers under the Constitution, thus intruding upon the sovereignty and authority of the States. . . .

To conclude that petitioner lacks standing to challenge a federal statute on grounds that the measure interferes with the powers reserved to States, the Court of Appeals relied on a single sentence from this Court's opinion in *Tennessee Elec. Power Co. v. TVA*, 306 U.S. 118 (1939).

[Yet, it] should be clear that *Tennessee Electric* does not cast doubt on Bond's standing for purposes of Article III's case-or-controversy requirement. This Court long ago disapproved of the case as authoritative respecting Article III limitations. [I]t is apparent—and in fact conceded not only by the Government but also by *amicus*—that Article III poses no barrier. One who seeks to initiate or continue proceedings in federal court must demonstrate, among other requirements, both standing to obtain the relief requested and, in addition, an "ongoing interest in the dispute" on the part of the opposing party that is sufficient to establish "concrete adverseness." When those conditions are met, Article III does not restrict the opposing party's ability to object to relief being sought at its expense. The requirement of Article III standing thus had no bearing upon Bond's capacity to assert defenses in the District Court. As for Bond's standing to appeal, it is clear Article III's prerequisites are met. Bond's challenge to her conviction and sentence "satisfies the case-or-controversy requirement, because the incarceration . . . constitutes a concrete injury, caused by the conviction and redressable by invalidation of the conviction."

To resolve the case, this Court must consider next whether *Tennessee Electric* is irrelevant with respect to prudential rules of standing as well. The question in *Tennessee Electric* was whether a group of private power companies could bring suit to enjoin the federally chartered Tennessee Valley Authority (TVA) from producing and selling electric power. It was conceded that competition from the TVA would "inflict substantial damage" upon the power companies. According to the companies, the federal statute authorizing the creation and operation of the TVA was invalid because, among other reasons, it exceeded the powers of the National Government in violation of the Tenth Amendment.

Declining to reach the merits, the Court concluded the power companies' lawsuit should be dismissed. It explained that the suit was premised on the principle that a person threatened with injury by conduct "which, but for statutory authority for its performance, would be a violation of his legal rights" could request an injunction from a court of equity and by this means test the validity of the statute. But the Court concluded that the TVA, even if it were shorn of congressional statutory authority, had done nothing more than compete as a supplier of electricity. And since state law did not purport to grant any of the power companies a monopoly, there was no basis for a suit in which the TVA might be forced to invoke its congressional authorization.

In that part of its analysis, and throughout its opinion, the *Tennessee Electric* Court stated that the problem with the power companies' suit was a lack of "standing" or a "cause of action." It treated those concepts as interchangeable.

Even though decisions since *Tennessee Electric* have been careful to use the terms "cause of action" and "standing" with more precision, the distinct concepts can be difficult to keep separate. If, for instance, the person alleging injury is remote from the zone of interests a statute protects, whether there is a legal injury at all and whether the particular litigant is one who may assert it can involve similar inquiries.

Still, the question whether a plaintiff states a claim for relief "goes to the merits" in the typical case, not the justiciability of a dispute, and conflation of the two concepts can cause confusion. This is the case with the Tenth Amendment discussion in *Tennessee Electric*. The *Tennessee Electric* Court noted that "[a] distinct ground upon which standing to maintain the suit is said to rest is that the acts of the Authority cannot be upheld without permitting federal regulation of purely local matters reserved to the states or the people by the Tenth Amendment." The Court rejected the argument, however, concluding the Tenth Amendment did not give one business a right to keep another from competing.

The Court then added the sentence upon which the Court of Appeals relied in the instant case, the sentence that has been the source of disagreement among Courts of Appeals: "As we have seen there is no objection to the Authority's operations by the states, and, if this were not so, the appellants, absent the states or their officers, have no standing in this suit to raise any question under the amendment." The quoted statement was in the context of a decision which held that business competitors had no legal injury, and the word standing can be interpreted in that sense. On this reading, the statement reiterated an earlier point. The statement explained that the States in which the TVA operated exempted it from their public utilities regulations; and that even if the States had not done so and the TVA had violated those regulations, the regulations were for the States to enforce. They conferred no private right of action on business competitors. . . .

Yet the quoted statement also could be read to refer to standing in the sense of whether the power companies were the proper litigants to raise a Tenth Amendment issue. To the extent that might have been the intention of the *Tennessee Electric* Court, it is, for reasons to be explained, inconsistent with our later precedents. The sentence from *Tennessee Electric* that we have quoted and discussed should be deemed neither controlling nor instructive on the issue of standing as that term is now defined and applied. . . .

The federal system rests on what might at first seem a counterintuitive insight, that "freedom is enhanced by the creation of two governments, not one." *Alden v. Maine*, 527 U.S. 706 (1999). The Framers concluded that allocation of powers between the National Government and the States enhances freedom, first by protecting the integrity of the governments themselves, and second by protecting the people, from whom all governmental powers are derived. . . .

Federalism is more than an exercise in setting the boundary between different institutions of government for their own integrity. "State sovereignty is not just an end in itself: 'Rather, federalism secures to citizens the liberties that derive from the diffusion of sovereign power.'" *New York v. United States*, 505 U.S. 144 (1992).

Some of these liberties are of a political character. The federal structure allows local policies "more sensitive to the diverse needs of a heterogeneous society," permits "innovation and experimentation," enables greater citizen "involvement in democratic processes," and makes government "more responsive by putting the States in competition for a mobile citizenry." *Gregory v. Ashcroft*, 501 U.S. 452 (1991). Federalism secures the freedom of the individual. It allows States to respond, through the enactment of positive law, to the initiative of those who seek a voice in shaping the destiny of their own times without having to rely solely upon the political processes that control a remote central power. True, of course, these objects cannot be vindicated by the Judiciary in the absence of a proper case or controversy; but the individual liberty secured by federalism is not simply derivative of the rights of the States.

Federalism also protects the liberty of all persons within a State by ensuring that laws enacted in excess of delegated governmental power cannot direct or control their actions. By denying any one government complete jurisdiction over all the concerns of public life, federalism protects the liberty of the individual from arbitrary power. When government acts in excess of its lawful powers, that liberty is at stake.

The limitations that federalism entails are not therefore a matter of rights belonging only to the States. States are not the sole intended beneficiaries of federalism. An individual has a direct interest in objecting to laws that upset the constitutional balance between the National Government and the States when the enforcement of those laws causes injury that is concrete, particular, and redressable. Fidelity to principles of federalism is not for the States alone to vindicate.

The recognition of an injured person's standing to object to a violation of a constitutional principle that allocates power within government is illustrated, in an analogous context, by cases in which individuals sustain discrete, justiciable injury from actions that transgress separation-of-powers limitations. Separation-of-powers principles are intended, in part, to protect each branch of government from incursion by the others. Yet the dynamic between and among the branches is not the only object of the Constitution's concern. The structural principles secured by the separation of powers protect the individual as well. . . .

There is no basis in precedent or principle to deny petitioner's standing to raise her claims. The ultimate issue of the statute's validity turns in part on whether the law can be deemed "necessary and proper for carrying into Execution" the President's Article II, Sec. 2 Treaty Power. This Court expresses no view on the merits of that argument. It can be addressed by the Court of Appeals on remand.

B | The Court's Docket and Screening Cases

■ INSIDE THE COURT

The Business of the Supreme Court in the 2010–2011 Term★

SUBJECT OF COURT OPINIONS	SUMMARY	PLENARY
Admiralty		
Antitrust		
Bankruptcy		2
Bill of Rights (other than rights of accused) and Equal Protection	1	6
Commerce Clause		
1. Constitutionality and construction of federal regulation		
2. Constitutionality of state regulation		1
Common Law		1
Miscellaneous Statutory Construction		19
Due process		
1. Economic interests		
2. Procedure and rights of accused	1	9
3. Substantive due process (noneconomic)		
Impairment of Contract and Just Compensation		
International Law, War, and Peace		
Jurisdiction, Procedure, and Practice	4	25
Land Legislation		
Native Americans	1	1
Patents, Copyright, and Trademarks	1	3
Other Suits against the Government		5
Suits by States		1
Taxation (federal and state)		2
Totals	**8**	**75**

★Note: The classification of cases is that of the author and necessarily invites differences of opinion as to the dominant issue in some cases. The table includes opinions in cases whether decided summarily or given plenary consideration, but not cases summarily disposed of by simple orders, opinions dissenting from the denial of review, and those dismissing cases as improvidently granted.

H | *Opinion Days and Communicating Decisions*

■ INSIDE THE COURT

*Opinion Writing during the 2010–2011 Term**

OPINIONS	MAJORITY	CONCURRING	DISSENTING	SEPARATE	TOTALS
Per Curiam	8				8
Roberts	7		4		11
Scalia	9	11	6	1	27
Kennedy	10	3	2		15
Thomas	10	9	5		24
Ginsburg	10	5	6	1	22
Breyer	7	6	9	1	23
Alito	8	6	4	1	19
Sotomayor	7	6	6		19
Kagan	7		2		9
Totals	83	46	45	4	177

*Note that court opinions disposing of two or more companion cases are counted only once here. In addition, this table includes opinions in cases disposed of either summarily or upon plenary consideration, but does not include cases summarily disposed of by simple orders, dismissed as improvidently granted, and concurring or dissenting opinions from the denial of *certiorari*.

3

PRESIDENTIAL POWER, THE RULE OF LAW, AND FOREIGN AFFAIRS

B | *As Commander in Chief and In Foreign Affairs*

In its 2011–2012 term the Court will consider the application of the "political question" doctrine and the boundaries between congressional and presidential power in *M. B. Z. v. Clinton* (Docket No. 10-699), which is further discussed here in Chapter 2.

4

The President as Chief Executive in Domestic Affairs

D | *Accountability and Immunities*

The Court granted review and will decide in its 2011–2012 term *Minneci v. Pollard* (10-1104), raising an important issue under the doctrine set forth in *Bivens v. Six Unknown Federal Narcotics Agents*, 403 U.S. 388 (1971). *Bivens* held that individuals may sue governmental officials for violating their constitutional rights, even if such suits are not authorized by federal statute. In *Bivens* the Court upheld a lawsuit seeking $15,000 in damages against six narcotics agents who forced their way into a New York City apartment without a warrant, threatened to arrest the entire family, and then took the father into custody. The father, Webster Bivens, claimed that he had no other remedy for this violation of his Fourth Amendment guarantee against unreasonable searches and seizures, and a majority of the Court agreed. Then, in *Davis v. Passman*, 442 U.S. 228 (1979), the Court allowed a *Bivens*-type lawsuit against a member of Congress for alleged sexual harassment of a staff member. And in *Carlson v. Green*, 446 U.S. 14 (1980), the Court permitted a mother to sue an officer of a prison after her prisoner son died, allegedly due to prison officials' failure to provide proper medical care for his asthma. Although the Court subsequently had numerous requests to further expand the range of *Bivens*-type lawsuits, it has refused to do so.

At issue in *Minneci v. Pollard* is whether private individuals working under government contract may be sued for violating individuals' constitutional rights. A three-judge panel of the Court of Appeals for the Ninth Circuit ruled in 2010 that a prison inmate, Richard Lee Pollard, could sue a group of contract employees working at a federal prison in California. Pollard claimed that he broke his elbow in a fall after tripping over a cart left in a hallway, but that prison guards nevertheless required him to use his arm in painful ways when taking him to and from an outside clinic for treatment, refused to provide a splint for the injury, and required him to return to his prison job before he had completely healed. The panel noted that "neither the Supreme Court nor our court has squarely addressed whether employees of a private corporation operating a prison under contract with the federal government act under color of federal law." Yet, the panel concluded that their actions should be treated as if they were federal employees. Over the dissent of eight judges, the Ninth Circuit refused to reconsider that ruling *en banc* and the Court granted review of the three-judge panel's decision.

7

THE STATES AND
AMERICAN FEDERALISM

In its 2011 term the Court will consider, in *Kurns v. Railroad Friction Products Corporation* (No. 10-879), whether the Federal Railroad Safety Act preempts railroad workers' personal injury claims under state tort law for failure to warn about hazardous substances released during the repair of locomotives. For 47 years, George Corson worked in repair shops removing insulation and brake shoes from locomotives. After retiring he was diagnosed with mesothelioma, the only known cause of which is exposure to asbestos—a component used in insulation and brake shoes. After filing a suit he died and his widow continued the lawsuit, claiming that his asbestos exposure was from boiler insulation and brake shoes. A federal district court granted a summary judgment for the defendants, holding that the tort claims were preempted by the Federal Railroad Safety Act and the Safety Appliance Act. The Court of Appeals for the Third Circuit affirmed, 620 F.3d 392 (3rd Cir., 2010), and that decision was appealed and the Court granted review.

A | *States' Power over Commerce and Regulation*

■ THE DEVELOPMENT OF LAW

Other Rulings on State Regulatory Powers in Alleged Conflict with Federal Legislation

CASE	VOTE	RULING
Bruesewitz v. Wyeth, 131 S.Ct. 1068 (2011)	6:2	Writing for the Court, Justice Scalia held that The National Childhood Vaccine Injury Act,

which created a no-fault program to compensate for vaccine-related injuries, preempts state laws and lawsuits over design-defect claims against vaccine manufacturers. Justices Sotomayor and Ginsburg dissented, and Justice Kagan did not participate.

Williamson v. Mazda Motor of America, 131 S.Ct. 1131 (2011)	8:0	Writing for the Court, Justice Breyer held that The Federal Motor Vehicle Safety Standard 208 does

not preempt state tort suits claiming that manufacturers should have installed lap-and-shoulder seat belts, instead of lap belts, on rear inner seats.

AT&T Mobility v. Concepcion, 131 S.Ct. 1740 (2011)	5:4	Writing for the majority, Justice Scalia held that California's "Discover Bank" regulation ran

counter to the purposes of Congress in enacting that legislation and thus was preempted. Justices Ginsburg, Breyer, Sotomayor, and Kagan dissented.

Chamber of Commerce v. Whiting, 131 S.Ct. 1968 (2011)	5:3	Writing for the Court, Chief Justice Roberts held that the 1986 Immigration Reform and Control Act did not preempt Arizona's 2007

law punishing businesses that hire illegal immigrants by enforcing "licensing and similar laws," including revoking their licenses. In doing so, Chief Justice Roberts rejected the argument that immigration was solely the province of the federal government and signaled that state and local governments may in some cases impose stricter restrictions and sanctions than under federal law. Justices Breyer, Ginsburg, and Sotomayor dissented, while Justice Kagan did not participate.

Pliva, Inc. v. Mensing, 131 S.Ct. 2567 (2011)	5:4	The Federal Drug Administra- tion recently strengthened re- quirements for warning labels

on prescription drugs—both name-brand and generic. Those regulations were challenged on the ground that drug manufacturers are also subject to state tort liability. Writing for the majority, Justice Thomas held that federal drug regulations requiring name-brand and generic drugs to have the same warning label preempts state tort law. Because state and federal laws address label warnings, the federal law is superior, and when it is impossible for a manufacturer to comply with both state and federal law, the federal law preempts conflicting state laws. Justices Ginsburg, Breyer, Sotomayor, and Kagan dissented.

B | *The Tenth and Eleventh Amendments and the States*

In its 2011–2012 term the Court will again consider the scope of the Eleventh Amendment, in *Coleman v. Maryland Court of Appeals* (No. 10-1016). At issue is whether Congress constitutionally abrogated the states' Eleventh Amendment immunity from lawsuits under the self-care provisions of the Family and Medical Leave Act.

■ THE DEVELOPMENT OF LAW

Other Recent Rulings on the Eleventh Amendment

CASE	VOTE	RULING
Sossamon v. Texas, 131 S.Ct. 1651 (2011)	6:2	While only noting in passing the Eleventh Amendment, Jus- tice Thomas held that state sover-

eignty, based on precedents and the structure of federalism, immunizes states from suits for monetary damages under the Religious Land Use and Insti-tutionalized Persons Act (RLUIPA). Justices Breyer and Sotomayor dissented, while Justice Kagan took no part in the decision.

8

REPRESENTATIVE GOVERNMENT, VOTING RIGHTS, AND ELECTORAL POLITICS

C | *Campaigns and Elections*

The Roberts Court revisited the controversy over public financing of campaigns for public office in *Arizona Free Enterprise Club's Freedom Club PAC v. Bennett* (2011) (excerpted below). In *Buckley v. Valeo*, 424 U.S. 1 (1976) (excerpted in Vol. 1, Ch. 8), the Burger Court upheld the transfer of taxpayer contributions (though a tax return checkoff) to presidential candidates willing to accept campaign spending limits in exchange for receiving public funding; both Presidents George W. Bush and Barack Obama declined in order to raise more money than the federal limits. In doing so, the Court reasoned that Congress had created a system "to reduce the deleterious influence of large contributions on our political process, to facilitate communication by candidates with the electorate, and to free candidates from the rigors of fund-raising." In *Davis v. Federal Election Commission*, 554 U.S. 724 (2008), however, the Roberts Court signaled a different predisposition. Although *Davis* did not involve public funding per se, but rather self-financed candidates, it considered the effects of candidates spending their own money. A bare majority struck down the so-called "millionaire's amendment," imposing limits on candidates' personal expenditures, to the Bipartisan Campaign Reform Act of 2002 (also known as "the McCain-Feingold law"). Notably, a bare majority of the Rehnquist Court invalidated other provisions of that law in *McConnell v. Federal Election Commission*, 540 U.S. 93 (2003) (excerpted in Vol. 1, Ch. 8), as did a bare majority of the Roberts Court when striking down its provisions forbidding corporations and unions from using general funds for direct contributions to candidates for certain federal offices, in *Citizens United v. Federal Election Commission*, 130 S.Ct. 876 (2010) (excerpted in Vol. 1, Ch. 8). Writing for the Court in *Davis*, Justice Alito held that the provision effectively imposed different contribution limits on competing candidates. Hence, Congress (not the voters) would determine whom to favor in an election and the differing restrictions put "a drag" on self-financed candidates' free speech. At issue in *Arizona Free Enterprise Club's Freedom Club PAC v. Bennett* was Arizona's law providing public subsidies for candidates who accept in exchange limits on campaign contributions and who would receive an additional subsidy if their self-financed opponent spent more than the state limits on campaign spending; in no event would self-financed candidates receive public funding.

Arizona Free Enterprise Club's Freedom Club PAC v. Bennett
131 S.Ct. 2806 (2011)

The constitutionality of Arizona's Clean Elections Act of 1998, which created a system of public campaign financing that subsidizes candidates for office, was challenged by several past and future candidates for office and political action committees. The law was adopted in a statewide initiative by a 51 to 49 percent margin, amid scandals over campaign financing that lead to the criminal prosecution of two governors and a number of state legislators. It created a subsidy scheme for races for governor, lieutenant governor, attorney general, state legislators, among other elected offices, and created a Citizens Clean Elections Commission to enforce the law. Under the statute, candidates may obtain public subsidies, though they may not pay for their campaigns entirely with public funds. They qualify for a subsidy if they raise a specified amount in private donations, provided that each contribution is no more than five dollars, and if their campaigns spend no more than the limits set by state law. Once they receive a subsidy they may no longer raise private funds and are limited to spending only the amount of the subsidy. However, there is also a "matching funds" provision, which was the focus of the challenge to the law. If a subsidized candidate has a "self-financed" opponent—who spends his or her own money or raises it from private contributions or political action committees—and spends more than the initial subsidy, then the subsidized candidate may receive an additional subsidy (but no more than twice the amount of the initial subsidy, and with six percent of the additional subsidy deducted to cover expenses). Moreover, if an independent group supports the subsidized candidate, the self-financed candidate receives no public funding. When the law went into effect in 2000, the matching-funds provision was challenged by several past and future would-be self-financed candidates and two political action committees that planned to support such candidates. A federal district court struck down the provision as a violation of the First Amendment. The Court of Appeals for the Ninth Circuit in turn reversed and upheld the matching-funds provision, upon concluding that the burden on self-financed candidates was minimal. Although the provision went into effect, challengers persuaded the Supreme Court to block the appellate court's decision upholding the provision in a June 2010 order. The challengers then filed petitions to the Court, which granted review.

The appellate court's decision was reversed. Chief Justice Roberts delivered the opinion for the Court. Justice Kagan filed a dissent, which Justices Ginsburg, Breyer, and Sotomayor joined.

☐ *CHIEF JUSTICE ROBERTS delivered the opinion of the Court.*

"Discussion of public issues and debate on the qualifications of candidates are integral to the operation" of our system of government. *Buckley v. Valeo*, 424 U.S. 1 (1976). As a result, the First Amendment "'has its fullest and most urgent application' to speech uttered during a campaign for political office." *Eu v. San Francisco County Democratic Central Comm.*, 489 U.S. 214 (1989). "Laws that burden political speech are" accordingly "subject to strict scrutiny, which requires the Government to prove that the restriction furthers a compelling interest and is narrowly tailored to achieve that interest." *Citizens United v. Federal Election Comm'n*, [130 S.Ct. 876] (2010).

Applying these principles, we have invalidated government-imposed restrictions on campaign expenditures, *Buckley*, restraints on independent expenditures applied to express advocacy groups, [*Federal Election Commission v.*] *Massachusetts Citizens for Life* [479 U.S. 238 (1986)], limits on uncoordinated political party expenditures, *Colorado Republican Federal Campaign Comm. v. Federal Election Comm'n*, 518 U.S. 604 (1996) (*Colorado I*), and regulations barring unions, nonprofit and other associations, and corporations from making independent expenditures for electioneering communication, *Citizens United*.

At the same time, we have subjected strictures on campaign-related speech that we have found less onerous to a lower level of scrutiny and upheld those restrictions. For example, after finding that the restriction at issue was "closely drawn" to serve a "sufficiently important interest," see, e.g., *McConnell v. Federal Election Comm'n*, 540 U.S. 93 (2003); *Nixon v. Shrink Missouri Government PA*, 528 U.S. 377 (2000), we have upheld government-imposed limits on contributions to candidates, *Buckley*, caps on coordinated party expenditures, *Federal Election Comm'n v. Colorado Republican Federal Campaign Comm.*, 533 U.S. 431 (2001) (*Colorado II*), and requirements that political funding sources disclose their identities, *Citizens United*.

Although the speech of the candidates and independent expenditure groups that brought this suit is not directly capped by Arizona's matching funds provision, those parties contend that their political speech is substantially burdened by the state law in the same way that speech was burdened by the law we recently found invalid in *Davis v. Federal Election Comm'n*, 554 U.S. 724 (2008). In *Davis*, we considered a First Amendment challenge to the so-called "Millionaire's Amendment" of the Bipartisan Campaign Reform Act of 2002. Under that Amendment, if a candidate for the United States House of Representatives spent more than $350,000 of his personal funds, "a new, asymmetrical regulatory scheme [came] into play." The opponent of the candidate who exceeded that limit was permitted to collect individual contributions up to $6,900 per contributor—three times the normal contribution limit of $2,300. The candidate who spent more than the personal funds limit remained subject to the original contribution cap. Davis argued that this scheme "burden[ed] his exercise of his First Amendment right to make unlimited expenditures of his personal funds because" doing so had "the effect of enabling his opponent to raise more money and to use that money to finance speech that counteract[ed] and thus diminishe[d] the effectiveness of Davis' own speech."

In addressing the constitutionality of the Millionaire's Amendment, we acknowledged that the provision did not impose an outright cap on a candidate's personal expenditures. We nonetheless concluded that the Amendment was unconstitutional because it forced a candidate "to choose between the First Amendment right to engage in unfettered political speech and subjection to discriminatory fundraising limitations." Any candidate who chose to spend more than $350,000 of his own money was forced to "shoulder a special and potentially significant burden" because that choice gave fundraising advantages to the candidate's adversary. We determined that this constituted an "unprecedented penalty" and "impose[d] a substantial burden on the exercise of the First Amendment right to use personal funds for campaign speech," and concluded that the Government had failed to advance any compelling interest that would justify such a burden.

The logic of *Davis* largely controls our approach to this case. Much like the burden placed on speech in *Davis*, the matching funds provision "imposes an unprecedented penalty on any candidate who robustly exercises [his] First Amendment right[s]."

Once a privately financed candidate has raised or spent more than the State's initial grant to a publicly financed candidate, each personal dollar spent by the privately financed candidate results in an award of almost one additional dollar to his opponent. That plainly forces the privately financed candidate to "shoulder a special and potentially significant burden" when choosing to exercise his First Amendment right to spend funds on behalf of his candidacy. If the law at issue in *Davis* imposed a burden on candidate speech, the Arizona law unquestionably does so as well.

The penalty imposed by Arizona's matching funds provision is different in some respects from the penalty imposed by the law we struck down in *Davis*. But those differences make the Arizona law more constitutionally problematic, not less. First, the penalty in *Davis* consisted of raising the contribution limits for one of the candidates. The candidate who benefited from the increased limits still had to go out and raise the funds. He may or may not have been able to do so. The other candidate, therefore, faced merely the possibility that his opponent would be able to raise additional funds, through contribution limits that remained subject to a cap. And still the Court held that this was an "unprecedented penalty," a "special and potentially significant burden" that had to be justified by a compelling state interest—a rigorous First Amendment hurdle. Here the benefit to the publicly financed candidate is the direct and automatic release of public money. That is a far heavier burden than in *Davis*.

Second, depending on the specifics of the election at issue, the matching funds provision can create a multiplier effect. [I]f the spending cap were exceeded, each dollar spent by the privately funded candidate would result in an additional dollar of campaign funding to each of that candidate's [multiple] publicly financed opponents. In such a situation, the matching funds provision forces privately funded candidates to fight a political hydra of sorts. Each dollar they spend generates two adversarial dollars in response. Again, a markedly more significant burden than in *Davis*.

Third, unlike the law at issue in *Davis*, all of this is to some extent out of the privately financed candidate's hands. Even if that candidate opted to spend less than the initial public financing cap, any spending by independent expenditure groups to promote the privately financed candidate's election—regardless whether such support was welcome or helpful—could trigger matching funds. . . .

The burdens that this regime places on independent expenditure groups are akin to those imposed on the privately financed candidates themselves. Just as with the candidate the independent group supports, the more money spent on that candidate's behalf or in opposition to a publicly funded candidate, the more money the publicly funded candidate receives from the State. And just as with the privately financed candidate, the effect of a dollar spent on election speech is a guaranteed financial payout to the publicly funded candidate the group opposes. Moreover, spending one dollar can result in the flow of dollars to multiple candidates the group disapproves of, dollars directly controlled by the publicly funded candidate or candidates. . . .

Arizona, the Clean Elections Institute, and the United States offer several arguments attempting to explain away the existence or significance of any burden imposed by matching funds. None is persuasive.

Arizona contends that the matching funds provision is distinguishable from the law we invalidated in *Davis*. The State correctly points out that our decision in *Davis* focused on the asymmetrical contribution limits imposed by the Millionaire's Amendment. But that is not because—as the State asserts—the reach of that opinion is limited to asymmetrical contribution limits. It is because that was the particular burden on candidate speech we faced in *Davis*.

The State argues that the matching funds provision actually results in more speech by "increas[ing] debate about issues of public concern" in Arizona elections and "promot[ing] the free and open debate that the First Amendment was intended to foster." In the State's view, this promotion of First Amendment ideals offsets any burden the law might impose on some speakers.

Not so. Any increase in speech resulting from the Arizona law is of one kind and one kind only—that of publicly financed candidates. The burden imposed on privately financed candidates and independent expenditure groups reduces their speech. Thus, even if the matching funds provision did result in more speech by publicly financed candidates and more speech in general, it would do so at the expense of impermissibly burdening (and thus reducing) the speech of privately financed candidates and independent expenditure groups. . . .

There is ample support for the argument that the matching funds provision seeks to "level the playing field" in terms of candidate resources. The clearest evidence is of course the very operation of the provision: It ensures that campaign funding is equal, up to three times the initial public funding allotment. The text of the Citizens Clean Elections Act itself confirms this purpose. The statutory provision setting up the matching funds regime is titled "Equal funding of candidates." The Act refers to the funds doled out after the Act's matching mechanism is triggered as "equalizing funds." And the regulations implementing the matching funds provision refer to those funds as "equalizing funds" as well. . . .

We have repeatedly rejected the argument that the government has a compelling state interest in "leveling the playing field" that can justify undue burdens on political speech. *Citizens United.* In *Davis*, we stated that discriminatory contribution limits meant to "level electoral opportunities for candidates of different personal wealth" did not serve "a legitimate government objective," let alone a compelling one. And in *Buckley*, we held that limits on overall campaign expenditures could not be justified by a purported government "interest in equalizing the financial resources of candidates." After all, equalizing campaign resources "might serve not to equalize the opportunities of all candidates, but to handicap a candidate who lacked substantial name recognition or exposure of his views before the start of the campaign."

"Leveling electoral opportunities means making and implementing judgments about which strengths should be permitted to contribute to the outcome of an election," *Davis,* —a dangerous enterprise and one that cannot justify burdening protected speech. The dissent essentially dismisses this concern, but it needs to be taken seriously; we have, as noted, held that it is not legitimate for the government to attempt to equalize electoral opportunities in this manner. And such basic intrusion by the government into the debate over who should govern goes to the heart of First Amendment values.

"Leveling the playing field" can sound like a good thing. But in a democracy, campaigning for office is not a game. It is a critically important form of speech. The First Amendment embodies our choice as a Nation that, when it comes to such speech, the guiding principle is freedom—the "unfettered interchange of ideas"—not whatever the State may view as fair. *Buckley.* . . .

We do not today call into question the wisdom of public financing as a means of funding political candidacy. That is not our business. But determining whether laws governing campaign finance violate the First Amendment is very much our business. In carrying out that responsibility over the past 35 years, we have upheld some restrictions on speech and struck down others.

We have said that governments "may engage in public financing of election campaigns" and that doing so can further "significant governmental interest[s]," such as the state interest in preventing corruption. *Buckley.* But the goal of creating a viable public financing scheme can only be pursued in a manner consistent with the First Amendment. The dissent criticizes the Court for standing in the way of what the people of Arizona want. But the whole point of the First Amendment is to protect speakers against unjustified government restrictions on speech, even when those restrictions reflect the will of the majority. When it comes to protected speech, the speaker is sovereign. . . .

The judgment of the Court of Appeals for the Ninth Circuit is reversed.

□ *Justice KAGAN, with whom Justice GINSBURG, Justice BREYER, and Justice SOTOMAYOR join, dissenting.*

Imagine two States, each plagued by a corrupt political system. In both States, candidates for public office accept large campaign contributions in exchange for the promise that, after assuming office, they will rank the donors' interests ahead of all others. As a result of these bargains, politicians ignore the public interest, sound public policy languishes, and the citizens lose confidence in their government.

Recognizing the cancerous effect of this corruption, voters of the first State, acting through referendum, enact several campaign finance measures previously approved by this Court. They cap campaign contributions; require disclosure of substantial donations; and create an optional public financing program that gives candidates a fixed public subsidy if they refrain from private fundraising. But these measures do not work. Individuals who "bundle" campaign contributions become indispensable to candidates in need of money. Simple disclosure fails to prevent shady dealing. And candidates choose not to participate in the public financing system because the sums provided do not make them competitive with their privately financed opponents. So the State remains afflicted with corruption.

Voters of the second State, having witnessed this failure, take an ever-so-slightly different tack to cleaning up their political system. They too enact contribution limits and disclosure requirements. But they believe that the greatest hope of eliminating corruption lies in creating an effective public financing program, which will break candidates' dependence on large donors and bundlers. These voters realize, based on the first State's experience, that such a program will not work unless candidates agree to participate in it. And candidates will participate only if they know that they will receive sufficient funding to run competitive races. So the voters enact a program that carefully adjusts the money given to would-be officeholders, through the use of a matching funds mechanism, in order to provide this assurance. The program does not discriminate against any candidate or point of view, and it does not restrict any person's ability to speak. In fact, by providing resources to many candidates, the program creates more speech and thereby broadens public debate. And just as the voters had hoped, the program accomplishes its mission of restoring integrity to the political system. The second State rids itself of corruption.

A person familiar with our country's core values—our devotion to democratic self-governance, as well as to "uninhibited, robust, and wide-open" debate, *New York Times Co. v. Sullivan*, 376 U.S. 254 (1964)—might expect this Court to celebrate, or at least not to interfere with, the second State's success. But today, the majority holds that the second State's system—the system that produces honest government, working on behalf of all the people—clashes with our Constitution. The First Amendment, the majority insists, requires us all to rely on the measures employed in the first State, even when they have failed to break the stranglehold of special interests on elected officials.

I disagree. The First Amendment's core purpose is to foster a healthy, vibrant political system full of robust discussion and debate. Nothing in Arizona's anti-corruption statute, the Arizona Citizens Clean Elections Act, violates this constitutional protection. To the contrary, the Act promotes the values underlying both the First Amendment and our entire Constitution by enhancing the "opportunity for free political discussion to the end that government may be responsive to the will of the people." I therefore respectfully dissent.

Campaign finance reform over the last century has focused on one key question: how to prevent massive pools of private money from corrupting our political system. If an officeholder owes his election to wealthy contributors, he may act for their benefit alone, rather than on behalf of all the people. As we recognized in *Buckley v. Valeo*, our seminal campaign finance case, large private contributions may result in "political quid pro quo[s]," which undermine the integrity of our democracy. And even if these contributions are not converted into corrupt bargains, they still may weaken confidence in our political system because the public perceives "the opportunities for abuse[s]." To prevent both corruption and the appearance of corruption—and so to protect our democratic system of governance—citizens have implemented reforms designed to curb the power of special interests.

Among these measures, public financing of elections has emerged as a potentially potent mechanism to preserve elected officials' independence. President Theodore Roosevelt proposed the reform as early as 1907 in his State of the Union address. "The need for collecting large campaign funds would vanish," he said, if the government "provided an appropriation for the proper and legitimate expenses" of running a campaign, on the condition that a "party receiving campaign funds from the Treasury" would forgo private fundraising. The idea was—and remains—straightforward. Candidates who rely on public, rather than private, moneys are "beholden [to] no person and, if elected, should feel no post-election obligation toward any contributor." By supplanting private cash in elections, public financing eliminates the source of political corruption.

For this reason, public financing systems today dot the national landscape. Almost one-third of the States have adopted some form of public financing, and so too has the Federal Government for presidential elections. The federal program—which offers presidential candidates a fixed public subsidy if they abstain from private fundraising—originated in the campaign finance law that Congress enacted in 1974 on the heels of the Watergate scandal. Congress explained at the time that the "potentia[l] for abuse" inherent in privately funded elections was "all too clear." In Congress's view, public financing represented the "only way . . . [to] eliminate reliance on large private contributions" and its attendant danger of corruption, while still ensuring that a wide range of candidates had access to the ballot.

We declared the presidential public financing system constitutional in *Buckley v. Valeo*. . . .

But this model, which distributes a lump-sum grant at the beginning of an election cycle, has a significant weakness: It lacks a mechanism for setting the subsidy at a level that will give candidates sufficient incentive to participate, while also conserving public resources. Public financing can achieve its goals only if a meaningful number of candidates receive the state subsidy, rather than raise private funds. But a public funding program must be voluntary to pass constitutional muster, because of its restrictions on contributions and expenditures. And candidates will choose to sign up only if the subsidy provided enables them to run competitive races. If the grant is pegged too low, it puts the participating candidate at a disadvantage: Because he has agreed to spend no more than the amount of the subsidy, he will lack the means to respond if his privately funded opponent spends over that threshold. So when lump-sum grants do not keep up with campaign expenditures, more and more candidates will choose not to participate. But if the subsidy is set too high, it may impose an unsustainable burden on the public fisc. At the least, hefty grants will waste public resources in the many state races where lack of competition makes such funding unnecessary.

The difficulty, then, is in finding the Goldilocks solution—not too large, not too small, but just right. And this in a world of countless variables—where the amount of money needed to run a viable campaign against a privately funded candidate depends on, among other things, the district, the office, and the election cycle. A state may set lump-sum grants district-by-district, based on spending in past elections; but even that approach leaves out many factors—including the resources of the privately funded candidate—that alter the competitiveness of a seat from one election to the next. In short, the dynamic nature of our electoral system makes *ex ante* predictions about campaign expenditures almost impossible. And that creates a chronic problem for lump-sum public financing programs, because inaccurate estimates produce subsidies that either dissuade candidates from participating or waste taxpayer money. And so States have made adjustments to the lump-sum scheme that we approved in *Buckley*, in attempts to more effectively reduce corruption.

The people of Arizona had every reason to try to develop effective anti-corruption measures. Before turning to public financing, Arizonans voted by referendum to establish campaign contribution limits. But that effort to abate corruption, standing alone, proved unsuccessful. Five years after the enactment of these limits, the State suffered "the worst public corruption scandal in its history." In that scandal, known as "AzScam," nearly 10% of the State's legislators were caught accepting campaign contributions or bribes in exchange for supporting a piece of legislation. Following that incident, the voters of Arizona decided that further reform was necessary. Acting once again by referendum, they adopted the public funding system at issue here.

The hallmark of Arizona's program is its inventive approach to the challenge that bedevils all public financing schemes: fixing the amount of the subsidy. For each electoral contest, the system calibrates the size of the grant automatically to provide sufficient—but no more than sufficient—funds to induce voluntary participation. In effect, the program's designers found the Goldilocks solution, which produces the "just right" grant to ensure that a participant in the system has the funds needed to run a competitive race.

As the Court explains, Arizona's matching funds arrangement responds to the shortcoming of the lump-sum model by adjusting the public subsidy in each race to reflect the expenditures of a privately financed candidate and the independent groups that support him. A publicly financed candidate in Arizona receives an initial lump-sum to get his campaign off the ground. But for every dollar his privately funded opponent (or the opponent's supporters) spends over the initial subsidy, the publicly funded candidate will—to a point—get an additional 94 cents. Once the publicly financed candidate has received three times the amount of the initial disbursement, he gets no further public funding, and remains barred from receiving private contributions, no matter how much more his privately funded opponent spends. This arrangement, like the lump-sum model, makes use of a pre-set amount to provide financial support to participants. For example, all publicly funded legislative candidates collect an initial grant of $21,479 for a general election race. And they can in no circumstances receive more than three times that amount ($64,437); after that, their privately funded competitors hold a marked advantage. But the Arizona system improves on the lump-sum model in a crucial respect. By tying public funding to private spending, the State can afford to set a more generous upper limit—because it knows that in each campaign it will only have to disburse what is necessary to keep a participating candidate reasonably competitive. Arizona can therefore assure candidates that, if they accept public funds, they will have the resources to run a viable race against those who rely on private money. And at the same time, Arizona avoids wasting taxpayers' dollars. In this way, the Clean Elections Act creates an effective and sustainable public financing system.

The question here is whether this modest adjustment to the public financing program that we approved in *Buckley* makes the Arizona law unconstitutional. The majority contends that the matching funds provision "substantially burdens protected political speech" and does not "serv[e] a compelling state interest." But the Court is wrong on both counts.

Arizona's statute does not impose a "restriction," or "substantia[l] burde[n]," on expression. The law has quite the opposite effect: It subsidizes and so produces more political speech. We recognized in *Buckley* that, for this reason, public financing of elections "facilitate[s] and enlarge[s] public discussion," in support of First Amendment values. And what we said then is just as true today. Except in a world gone topsy-turvy, additional campaign speech and electoral competition is not a First Amendment injury.

At every turn, the majority tries to convey the impression that Arizona's matching fund statute is of a piece with laws prohibiting electoral speech. The majority invokes the language of "limits," "bar[s]," and "restraints." It equates the law to a "restrictio[n] on the amount of money a person or group can spend on political communication during a campaign." It insists that the statute "restrict[s] the speech of some elements of our society" to enhance the speech of others. And it concludes by reminding us that the point of the First Amendment is to protect "against unjustified government restrictions on speech."

There is just one problem. Arizona's matching funds provision does not restrict, but instead subsidizes, speech. . . .

And under the First Amendment, that makes all the difference. In case after case, year upon year, we have distinguished between speech restrictions and speech subsidies. "'There is a basic difference,'" we have held, "'between direct state interference with [First Amendment] protected activity and state encouragement'" of other expression. *Rust v. Sullivan*, 500 U.S. 173 (1991). That is because subsidies, by definition and contra the majority, do not restrict any speech.

No one can claim that Arizona's law discriminates against particular ideas, and so violates the First Amendment's sole limitation on speech subsidies. The State throws open the doors of its public financing program to all candidates who meet minimal eligibility requirements and agree not to raise private funds. Republicans and Democrats, conservatives and liberals may participate; so too, the law applies equally to independent expenditure groups across the political spectrum. Arizona disburses funds based not on a candidate's (or supporter's) ideas, but on the candidate's decision to sign up for public funding. So under our precedent, Arizona's subsidy statute should easily survive First Amendment scrutiny. . . .

The majority has one, and only one, way of separating this case from *Buckley* and our other, many precedents involving speech subsidies. According to the Court, the special problem here lies in Arizona's matching funds mechanism, which the majority claims imposes a "substantia[l] burde[n]" on a privately funded candidate's speech. Sometimes, the majority suggests that this "burden" lies in the way the mechanism "'diminish[es] the effectiveness'" of the privately funded candidate's expression by enabling his opponent to respond. At other times, the majority indicates that the "burden" resides in the deterrent effect of the mechanism: The privately funded candidate "might not spend money" because doing so will trigger matching funds. Either way, the majority is wrong to see a substantial burden on expression.

Most important, and as just suggested, the very notion that additional speech constitutes a "burden" is odd and unsettling. Here is a simple fact:

Arizona imposes nothing remotely resembling a coercive penalty on privately funded candidates. The State does not jail them, fine them, or subject them to any kind of lesser disability. The only "burden" in this case comes from the grant of a subsidy to another person, and the opportunity that subsidy allows for responsive speech. . . .

But put to one side this most fundamental objection to the majority's argument; even then, has the majority shown that the burden resulting from the Arizona statute is "substantial"? I will not quarrel with the majority's assertion that responsive speech by one candidate may make another candidate's speech less effective; that, after all, is the whole idea of the First Amendment, and a benefit of having more responsive speech. And I will assume that the operation of this statute may on occasion deter a privately funded candidate from spending money, and conveying ideas by that means. My guess is that this does not happen often: Most political candidates, I suspect, have enough faith in the power of their ideas to prefer speech on both sides of an issue to speech on neither. But I will take on faith that the matching funds provision may lead one or another privately funded candidate to stop spending at one or another moment in an election. Still, does that effect count as a severe burden on expression? By the measure of our prior decisions—which have upheld campaign reforms with an equal or greater impact on speech—the answer is no.

Number one: Any system of public financing, including the lump-sum model upheld in *Buckley* imposes a similar burden on privately funded candidates. . . .

Number two: Our decisions about disclosure and disclaimer requirements show the Court is wrong. Starting in *Buckley* and continuing through last Term, the Court has repeatedly declined to view these requirements as a substantial First Amendment burden, even though they discourage some campaign speech. "It is undoubtedly true," we stated in *Buckley*, that public disclosure obligations "will deter some individuals" from engaging in expressive activity. Yet we had no difficulty upholding these requirements there. And much more recently, in *Citizens United* and *Doe v. Reed*, [130 S.Ct. 486] (2010), we followed that precedent. "Disclosure requirements may burden the ability to speak," we reasoned, but they "do not prevent anyone from speaking." So too here. Like a disclosure rule, the matching funds provision may occasionally deter, but "impose[s] no ceiling" on electoral expression. . . .

For all these reasons, the Court errs in holding that the government action in this case substantially burdens speech and so requires the State to offer a compelling interest. But in any event, Arizona has come forward with just such an interest, explaining that the Clean Elections Act attacks corruption and the appearance of corruption in the State's political system. The majority's denigration of this interest—the suggestion that it either is not real or does not matter—wrongly prevents Arizona from protecting the strength and integrity of its democracy. . . .

This case arose because Arizonans wanted their government to work on behalf of all the State's people. On the heels of a political scandal involving the near-routine purchase of legislators' votes, Arizonans passed a law designed to sever political candidates' dependence on large contributors. They wished, as many of their fellow Americans wish, to stop corrupt dealing—to ensure that their representatives serve the public, and not just the wealthy donors who helped put them in office. The legislation that Arizona's voters enacted was the product of deep thought and care. It put into effect a public financing system that attracted large numbers of candidates at a sustainable cost to the State's taxpayers. The system discriminated against no ideas and prevented no speech. Indeed, by increasing electoral competition and enabling a wide range of candidates to express their views, the system "further[ed] . . . First Amendment values." *Buckley.* Less corruption, more speech. Robust campaigns leading to the election of representatives not beholden to the few, but accountable to the many. The people of Arizona might have expected a decent respect for those objectives.

Today, they do not get it. The Court invalidates Arizonans' efforts to ensure that in their State, "'[t]he people . . . possess the absolute sovereignty.'" No precedent compels the Court to take this step; to the contrary, today's decision is in tension with broad swaths of our First Amendment doctrine. No fundamental principle of our Constitution backs the Court's ruling; to the contrary, it is the law struck down today that fostered both the vigorous competition of ideas and its ultimate object—a government responsive to the will of the people. Arizonans deserve better. Like citizens across this country, Arizonans deserve a government that represents and serves them all. And no less, Arizonans deserve the chance to reform their electoral system so as to attain that most American of goals.

Truly, democracy is not a game. I respectfully dissent.

■ The Development of Law

Other Rulings on Campaigns and Elections

CASE	VOTE	RULING
Nevada Commission on Ethics v. Carrington, 131 S.Ct. 857 (2011)	9:0	Nevada's Ethics in Government Law requires public officials to recuse themselves "from voting on, or advocating the passage or

failure of 'a matter with respect to which the independence of judgment of a reasonable person in his situation would be materially affected by' . . . '[h]is commitment in a private capacity to the interests of others.'" The commission investigated an elected local official, who had voted to approve a hotel/casino project proposed by a company that used his long-time friend and campaign manager as a paid consultant, and concluded he should have recused himself and therefore censured him. The official challenged that decision and the state supreme court held that the law was overly broad and ran afoul of the First Amendment. Writing for the Court, Justice Scalia reversed and held that the law was not unconstitutional but a "reasonable time, place, and manner" limitation.

SUPREME COURT WATCH 2011

VOLUME TWO

4

THE NATIONALIZATION

OF THE

BILL OF RIGHTS

B │ *The Rise and (Partial) Retreat of the "Due Process Revolution"*

■ THE DEVELOPMENT OF LAW

Other Recent Rulings on Substantive and Procedural Due Process

---

CASE	VOTE	RULING
District Attorney's Office for Third Judicial District v. Osborne, 129 S.Ct. 2308 (2009)	5:4	Writing for the Court, Chief Justice Roberts rejected a *substantive due process* claim to file a Section 1983 lawsuit against state officials

for violating a constitutional right of access to the result of DNA testing that was used as evidence at trial. In doing so, the chief justice emphasized that states were developing their own standards for the introduction and access to DNA evidence and that there was no need to constitutionalize the matter. Justices Stevens, Souter, Ginsburg, and Breyer dissented.

Skinner v. Switzer, 131 S.Ct.   6:3   Distinguishing the ruling in *District Attorney's Office v. Osborne,* 129 S.Ct. 2308 (2009), the Court held that Texas's denial of all DNA evidence, specifically unused evidence at trial, to a death-row inmate violated procedural due process and thus permits Section 1983 civil rights suits. Writing for the Court, Justice Ginsburg emphasized the narrowness of the holding and that it leaves "slim room" to bring such challenges. By contrast, the dissenters—Justices Kennedy, Thomas, and Alito—protested that the ruling provided a "roadmap" for state inmates to reopen DNA-access claims after having lost in *habeas corpus* appeals, and therefore opened the "floodgate" for such lawsuits.

Turner v. Rogers, 131 S.Ct.   5:4   Writing for the Court, Justice Breyer held that due process does not require states to provide attorneys for indigents in civil proceedings, even if they may result in incarceration for willful contempt in repeatedly failing to make child-support payments. However, the majority ruled that in such proceedings states should provide "substitute procedural safeguards," such as (1) notice to the defendant that his ability to pay is a critical issue in contempt proceedings; (2) the use of a form to elicit relevant financial information; (3) an opportunity at the hearing to respond to statements and questions about financial status; and (4) an express finding by the court that the defendant has the ability to pay. Chief Justice Roberts and Justices Scalia, Thomas, and Alito dissented.

5

FREEDOM OF EXPRESSION
AND ASSOCIATION

A | *Judicial Approaches to the First Amendment*

---

(2) *Judicial Line Drawing: Ad hoc* and Definitional Balancing

By a seven-to-two vote in *Brown v. Entertainment Merchants Association* (excerpted below), the Court struck down California's law punishing the sales of violent video games to minors. Justice Scalia's opinion for the Court swept broadly in reaffirming the broad protection of the First Amendment and refusing to carve out another category of unprotected speech. Justice Alito, joined by Chief Justice Roberts, concurred but left open the possibility of upholding such a law if properly framed. Justices Thomas and Breyer dissented. Notably, Justice Thomas would have upheld the law based on the "original understanding" of freedom of speech, while Justice Breyer would have done so based on social science data and the projected consequences of violent video games.

Brown v. Entertainment Merchants Association
131 S.Ct. 2729 (2011)

In 2005, California enacted a law requiring the labeling of video games containing violence and the sales of such videos to minors, with up to $1,000 for violations. When the constitutionality of the law was challenged, the state argued for the extension of a constitutional standard, created for cases involving the protection of minors from obscene materials, to violent materials, rather than obscenity. That standard derives from *Ginsberg v. New York*, 390 U.S. 629 (1968), The statute defines a violent video game as one depicting the "killing, maiming, dismembering, or sexually assaulting the image of a human being" in a manner that a reasonable person would find appeals to "a deviant or morbid interest" of minors, and is "patently offensive" to prevailing standards of what is suitable for minors and causes the game—as a whole—to lack "serious, artistic, political or scientific value" for minors. A federal district court, however, blocked the enforcement of the law. On appeal, the Court of Appeals for the Ninth Circuit found the statute to run afoul of the First Amendment, rejecting the proposed extension of the *Ginsberg* standard and using instead the "strict scrutiny" test. It held that there was no proof that playing such games harms, physically or psychologically, minors. The state appealed and the Court granted review.

The appellate court's decision was affirmed by a seven to two vote. Justice Scalia delivered the opinion for the Court. Justice Alito filed a concurrence, joined by Chief Justice Roberts. Justices Thomas and Breyer each issued dissenting opinions.

□ *Justice SCALIA delivered the opinion of the Court.*

Like the protected books, plays, and movies that preceded them, video games communicate ideas—and even social messages—through many familiar literary devices (such as characters, dialogue, plot, and music) and through features distinctive to the medium (such as the player's interaction with the virtual world). That suffices to confer First Amendment protection. Under our Constitution, "esthetic and moral judgments about art and literature . . . are for the individual to make, not for the Government to decree, even with the mandate or approval of a majority." *United States v. Playboy Entertainment Group, Inc.*, 529 U.S. 803 (2000). And whatever the challenges of applying the Constitution to ever-advancing technology, "the basic principles of freedom of speech and the press, like the First Amendment's command, do not vary" when a new and different medium for communication appears. *Joseph Burstyn, Inc. v. Wilson*, 343 U.S. 495 (1952).

The most basic of those principles is this: "[A]s a general matter, . . . government has no power to restrict expression because of its message, its ideas, its subject matter, or its content." *Ashcroft v. American Civil Liberties Union*, 535

U.S. 564 (2002). There are of course exceptions. "'From 1791 to the present,'. . . the First Amendment has 'permitted restrictions upon the content of speech in a few limited areas,' and has never 'include[d] a freedom to disregard these traditional limitations.'" *United States v. Stevens*, [130 S.Ct. 1577] (2010). These limited areas—such as obscenity, *Roth v. United States*, 354 U.S. 476 483 (1957), incitement, *Brandenburg v. Ohio*, 395 U.S. 444 (1969), and fighting words, *Chaplinsky v. New Hampshire*, 315 U.S. 568 (1942)—represent "well-defined and narrowly limited classes of speech, the prevention and punishment of which have never been thought to raise any Constitutional problem."

Last Term, in *Stevens*, we held that new categories of unprotected speech may not be added to the list by a legislature that concludes certain speech is too harmful to be tolerated. *Stevens* concerned a federal statute purporting to criminalize the creation, sale, or possession of certain depictions of animal cruelty. . . .

That holding controls this case. As in *Stevens*, California has tried to make violent-speech regulation look like obscenity regulation by appending a saving clause required for the latter. That does not suffice. Our cases have been clear that the obscenity exception to the First Amendment does not cover whatever a legislature finds shocking, but only depictions of "sexual conduct," *Miller* [*v. California*, 413 U.S. 15 (1973)]. . . .

Because speech about violence is not obscene, it is of no consequence that California's statute mimics the New York statute regulating obscenity-for-minors that we upheld in *Ginsberg v. New York*, 390 U.S. 629 (1968). That case approved a prohibition on the sale to minors of sexual material that would be obscene from the perspective of a child. We held that the legislature could "adjus[t] the definition of obscenity 'to social realities by permitting the appeal of this type of material to be assessed in terms of the sexual interests . . .' of . . . minors." And because "obscenity is not protected expression," the New York statute could be sustained so long as the legislature's judgment that the proscribed materials were harmful to children "was not irrational."

The California Act is something else entirely. It does not adjust the boundaries of an existing category of unprotected speech to ensure that a definition designed for adults is not uncritically applied to children. California does not argue that it is empowered to prohibit selling offensively violent works to adults—and it is wise not to, since that is but a hair's breadth from the argument rejected in *Stevens*. Instead, it wishes to create a wholly new category of content-based regulation that is permissible only for speech directed at children.

That is unprecedented and mistaken. "[M]inors are entitled to a significant measure of First Amendment protection, and only in relatively narrow and well-defined circumstances may government bar public dissemination of protected materials to them." *Erznoznik v. Jacksonville*, 422 U.S. 205 (1975). No doubt a State possesses legitimate power to protect children from harm, but that does not include a free-floating power to restrict the ideas to which children may be exposed. "Speech that is neither obscene as to youths nor subject to some other legitimate proscription cannot be suppressed solely to protect the young from ideas or images that a legislative body thinks unsuitable for them." *Erznoznik*. . . .

California's argument would fare better if there were a longstanding tradition in this country of specially restricting children's access to depictions of violence, but there is none. Certainly the books we give children to read—or read to them when they are younger—contain no shortage of gore. *Grimm's*

Fairy Tales, for example, are grim indeed. As her just deserts for trying to poison Snow White, the wicked queen is made to dance in red hot slippers "till she fell dead on the floor, a sad example of envy and jealousy." Cinderella's evil stepsisters have their eyes pecked out by doves. And Hansel and Gretel (children!) kill their captor by baking her in an oven.

High-school reading lists are full of similar fare. Homer's Odysseus blinds Polyphemus the Cyclops by grinding out his eye with a heated stake. . . . And Golding's *Lord of the Flies* recounts how a schoolboy called Piggy is savagely murdered by other children while marooned on an island.

This is not to say that minors' consumption of violent entertainment has never encountered resistance. In the 1800's, dime novels depicting crime and "penny dreadfuls" (named for their price and content) were blamed in some quarters for juvenile delinquency. When motion pictures came along, they became the villains instead. For a time, our Court did permit broad censorship of movies because of their capacity to be "used for evil," but we eventually reversed course. *Joseph Burstyn, Inc.* Radio dramas were next, and then came comic books. Many in the late 1940's and early 1950's blamed comic books for fostering a "preoccupation with violence and horror" among the young, leading to a rising juvenile crime rate.

California claims that video games present special problems because they are "interactive," in that the player participates in the violent action on screen and determines its outcome. The latter feature is nothing new: Since at least the publication of *The Adventures of You: Sugarcane Island* in 1969, young readers of choose-your-own-adventure stories have been able to make decisions that determine the plot by following instructions about which page to turn to. . . .

Because the Act imposes a restriction on the content of protected speech, it is invalid unless California can demonstrate that it passes strict scrutiny—that is, unless it is justified by a compelling government interest and is narrowly drawn to serve that interest. The State must specifically identify an "actual problem" in need of solving, and the curtailment of free speech must be actually necessary to the solution. That is a demanding standard. "It is rare that a regulation restricting speech because of its content will ever be permissible."

California cannot meet that standard. At the outset, it acknowledges that it cannot show a direct causal link between violent video games and harm to minors. Rather, relying upon our decision in *Turner Broadcasting System, Inc. v. FCC*, 512 U.S. 622 (1994), the State claims that it need not produce such proof because the legislature can make a predictive judgment that such a link exists, based on competing psychological studies. But reliance on *Turner Broadcasting* is misplaced. That decision applied intermediate scrutiny to a content-neutral regulation. California's burden is much higher, and because it bears the risk of uncertainty, ambiguous proof will not suffice.

The State's evidence is not compelling. California relies primarily on the research of Dr. Craig Anderson and a few other research psychologists whose studies purport to show a connection between exposure to violent video games and harmful effects on children. These studies have been rejected by every court to consider them, and with good reason: They do not prove that violent video games cause minors to act aggressively (which would at least be a beginning). Instead, "[n]early all of the research is based on correlation, not evidence of causation, and most of the studies suffer from significant, admitted flaws in methodology." They show at best some correlation between exposure to violent entertainment and minuscule real-world effects, such as children's feeling more aggressive or making louder noises in the few minutes after playing a violent game than after playing a nonviolent game. . . .

The Act is also seriously underinclusive in another respect—and a respect that renders irrelevant the contentions of the concurrence and the dissents that video games are qualitatively different from other portrayals of violence. The California Legislature is perfectly willing to leave this dangerous, mind-altering material in the hands of children so long as one parent (or even an aunt or uncle) says it's OK. And there are not even any requirements as to how this parental or avuncular relationship is to be verified; apparently the child's or putative parent's, aunt's, or uncle's say-so suffices. That is not how one addresses a serious social problem. . . .

California's legislation straddles the fence between (1) addressing a serious social problem and (2) helping concerned parents control their children. Both ends are legitimate, but when they affect First Amendment rights they must be pursued by means that are neither seriously underinclusive nor seriously overinclusive. See *Church of Lukumi Babalu Aye, Inc. v. Hialeah*, 508 U.S. 520 (1993). As a means of protecting children from portrayals of violence, the legislation is seriously underinclusive, not only because it excludes portrayals other than video games, but also because it permits a parental or avuncular veto. And as a means of assisting concerned parents it is seriously overinclusive because it abridges the First Amendment rights of young people whose parents (and aunts and uncles) think violent video games are a harmless pastime. And the overbreadth in achieving one goal is not cured by the underbreadth in achieving the other. Legislation such as this, which is neither fish nor fowl, cannot survive strict scrutiny.

☐ *Justice ALITO, with whom THE CHIEF JUSTICE joins, concurring in the judgment.*

The California statute that is before us in this case represents a pioneering effort to address what the state legislature and others regard as a potentially serious social problem: the effect of exceptionally violent video games on impressionable minors, who often spend countless hours immersed in the alternative worlds that these games create. Although the California statute is well intentioned, its terms are not framed with the precision that the Constitution demands, and I therefore agree with the Court that this particular law cannot be sustained.

I disagree, however, with the approach taken in the Court's opinion. In considering the application of unchanging constitutional principles to new and rapidly evolving technology, this Court should proceed with caution. We should make every effort to understand the new technology. We should take into account the possibility that developing technology may have important societal implications that will become apparent only with time. We should not jump to the conclusion that new technology is fundamentally the same as some older thing with which we are familiar. And we should not hastily dismiss the judgment of legislators, who may be in a better position than we are to assess the implications of new technology. The opinion of the Court exhibits none of this caution. . . .

There are reasons to suspect that the experience of playing violent video games just might be very different from reading a book, listening to the radio, or watching a movie or a television show. . . .

Here, the California law does not define "violent video games" with the "narrow specificity" that the Constitution demands. In an effort to avoid First

Amendment problems, the California Legislature modeled its violent video game statute on the New York law that this Court upheld in *Ginsberg v. New York*, 390 U.S. 629 (1968)—a law that prohibited the sale of certain sexually related materials to minors. But the California Legislature departed from the *Ginsberg* model in an important respect, and the legislature overlooked important differences between the materials falling within the scope of the two statutes. . . .

Although our society does not generally regard all depictions of violence as suitable for children or adolescents, the prevalence of violent depictions in children's literature and entertainment creates numerous opportunities for reasonable people to disagree about which depictions may excite "deviant" or "morbid" impulses.

Finally, the difficulty of ascertaining the community standards incorporated into the California law is compounded by the legislature's decision to lump all minors together. The California law draws no distinction between young children and adolescents who are nearing the age of majority.

For these reasons, I conclude that the California violent video game law fails to provide the fair notice that the Constitution requires. And I would go no further. I would not express any view on whether a properly drawn statute would or would not survive First Amendment scrutiny. We should address that question only if and when it is necessary to do so.

[I] will now briefly elaborate on my reasons for questioning the wisdom of the Court's approach. Some of these reasons are touched upon by the dissents, and while I am not prepared at this time to go as far as either Justice THOMAS or Justice BREYER, they raise valid concerns.

The Court is wrong in saying that the holding in *United States v. Stevens*, [130 S.Ct. 1577] (2010), "controls this case." First, the statute in *Stevens* differed sharply from the statute at issue here. *Stevens* struck down a law that broadly prohibited any person from creating, selling, or possessing depictions of animal cruelty for commercial gain. The California law involved here, by contrast, is limited to the sale or rental of violent video games to minors. The California law imposes no restriction on the creation of violent video games, or on the possession of such games by anyone, whether above or below the age of 18.

Second, *Stevens* does not support the proposition that a law like the one at issue must satisfy strict scrutiny. The portion of *Stevens* on which the Court relies rejected the Government's contention that depictions of animal cruelty were categorically outside the range of any First Amendment protection. Going well beyond *Stevens*, the Court now holds that any law that attempts to prevent minors from purchasing violent video games must satisfy strict scrutiny instead of the more lenient standard applied in *Ginsberg*, our most closely related precedent. As a result of today's decision, a State may prohibit the sale to minors of what *Ginsberg* described as "girlie magazines," but a State must surmount a formidable (and perhaps insurmountable) obstacle if it wishes to prevent children from purchasing the most violent and depraved video games imaginable.

Third, *Stevens* expressly left open the possibility that a more narrowly drawn statute targeting depictions of animal cruelty might be compatible with the First Amendment. In this case, the Court's sweeping opinion will likely be read by many, both inside and outside the video-game industry, as suggesting that no regulation of minors' access to violent video games is allowed—at least without supporting evidence that may not be realistically obtainable given the nature of the phenomenon in question. . . .

Finally, the Court is far too quick to dismiss the possibility that the experience of playing video games (and the effects on minors of playing violent video games) may be very different from anything that we have seen before. Any assessment of the experience of playing video games must take into account certain characteristics of the video games that are now on the market and those that are likely to be available in the near future.

Today's most advanced video games create realistic alternative worlds in which millions of players immerse themselves for hours on end. These games feature visual imagery and sounds that are strikingly realistic, and in the near future video-game graphics may be virtually indistinguishable from actual video footage. Many of the games already on the market can produce high definition images, and it is predicted that it will not be long before video-game images will be seen in three dimensions. It is also forecast that video games will soon provide sensory feedback. By wearing a special vest or other device, a player will be able to experience physical sensations supposedly felt by a character on the screen. Some *amici* who support respondents foresee the day when "'virtual-reality shoot-'em-ups'" will allow children to "'actually feel the splatting blood from the blown-off head'" of a victim. . . .

In some of these games, the violence is astounding. Victims by the dozens are killed with every imaginable implement, including machine guns, shotguns, clubs, hammers, axes, swords, and chainsaws. Victims are dismembered, decapitated, disemboweled, set on fire, and chopped into little pieces. They cry out in agony and beg for mercy. Blood gushes, splatters, and pools. Severed body parts and gobs of human remains are graphically shown. . . .

If the technological characteristics of the sophisticated games that are likely to be available in the near future are combined with the characteristics of the most violent games already marketed, the result will be games that allow troubled teens to experience in an extraordinarily personal and vivid way what it would be like to carry out unspeakable acts of violence.

The Court is untroubled by this possibility. . . .

For all these reasons, I would hold only that the particular law at issue here fails to provide the clear notice that the Constitution requires. . . . If differently framed statutes are enacted by the States or by the Federal Government, we can consider the constitutionality of those laws when cases challenging them are presented to us.

□ *Justice THOMAS, dissenting.*

The Court's decision today does not comport with the original public understanding of the First Amendment. The majority strikes down, as facially unconstitutional, a state law that prohibits the direct sale or rental of certain video games to minors because the law "abridg[es] the freedom of speech." But I do not think the First Amendment stretches that far. The practices and beliefs of the founding generation establish that "the freedom of speech," as originally understood, does not include a right to speak to minors (or a right of minors to access speech) without going through the minors' parents or guardians. I would hold that the law at issue is not facially unconstitutional under the First Amendment, and reverse and remand for further proceedings.

When interpreting a constitutional provision, "the goal is to discern the most likely public understanding of [that] provision at the time it was adopted." *McDonald v. Chicago*, [130 S.Ct. 1037] (2010) (THOMAS, J., concurring in part and concurring in judgment). Because the Constitution is a written instrument, "its meaning does not alter." *McIntyre v. Ohio Elections Comm'n*, 514 U.S. 334 (1995) (THOMAS, J., concurring in judgment).

As originally understood, the First Amendment's protection against laws "abridging the freedom of speech" did not extend to all speech. "There are certain well-defined and narrowly limited classes of speech, the prevention and punishment of which have never been thought to raise any Constitutional problem." *Chaplinsky v. New Hampshire*, 315 U.S. 568 (1942). Laws regulating such speech do not "abridg[e] the freedom of speech" because such speech is understood to fall outside "the freedom of speech."

In my view, the "practices and beliefs held by the Founders" reveal another category of excluded speech: speech to minor children bypassing their parents. The historical evidence shows that the founding generation believed parents had absolute authority over their minor children and expected parents to use that authority to direct the proper development of their children. It would be absurd to suggest that such a society understood "the freedom of speech" to include a right to speak to minors (or a corresponding right of minors to access speech) without going through the minors' parents. The founding generation would not have considered it an abridgment of "the freedom of speech" to support parental authority by restricting speech that bypasses minors' parents.

Attitudes toward children were in a state of transition around the time that the States ratified the Bill of Rights. A complete understanding of the founding generation's views on children and the parent-child relationship must therefore begin roughly a century earlier, in colonial New England.

In the Puritan tradition common in the New England Colonies, fathers ruled families with absolute authority. The Puritans rejected many customs, such as godparenthood, that they considered inconsistent with the patriarchal structure.

Part of the father's absolute power was the right and duty "to fill his children's minds with knowledge and . . . make them apply their knowledge in right action." . . .

This conception of parental authority was reflected in laws at that time. In the Massachusetts Colony, for example, it was unlawful for tavern keepers (or anyone else) to entertain children without their parents' consent. . . .

In the decades leading up to and following the Revolution, attitudes towards children changed. Children came to be seen less as innately sinful and more as blank slates requiring careful and deliberate development. But the same overarching principles remained. Parents continued to have both the right and duty to ensure the proper development of their children. They exercised significant authority over their children, including control over the books that children read. And laws at the time continued to reflect strong support for parental authority and the sense that children were not fit to govern themselves.

The works of John Locke and Jean-Jacques Rousseau were a driving force behind the changed understanding of children and childhood. Locke taught that children's minds were blank slates and that parents therefore had to be careful and deliberate about what their children were told and observed. Parents had only themselves to blame if, "by humouring and cockering" their children, they "poison'd the fountain" and later "taste[d] the bitter waters." *Some Thoughts Concerning Education* (1692). Rousseau disagreed with Locke in important respects, but his philosophy was similarly premised on parental control over a child's development. Although Rousseau advocated that children should be allowed to develop naturally, he instructed that the environment be directed by "a tutor who is given total control over the child and who removes him from society, from all competing sources of authority and influence." . . .

Locke's and Rousseau's writings fostered a new conception of childhood. Children were increasingly viewed as malleable creatures, and childhood came to be seen as an important period of growth, development, and preparation for adulthood. . . .

The Revolution only amplified these concerns. The Republic would require virtuous citizens, which necessitated proper training from childhood.

Based on these views of childhood, the founding generation understood parents to have a right and duty to govern their children's growth. Parents were expected to direct the development and education of their children and ensure that bad habits did not take root.

This conception of parental rights and duties was exemplified by Thomas Jefferson's approach to raising children. He wrote letters to his daughters constantly and often gave specific instructions about what the children should do. . . .

The concept of total parental control over children's lives extended into the schools. . . . Adults carefully controlled what they published for children. Stories written for children were dedicated to moral instruction and were relatively austere, lacking details that might titillate children's minds. . . . Parents had total authority over what their children read. . . .

The law at the time reflected the founding generation's understanding of parent-child relations. According to Sir William Blackstone, parents were responsible for maintaining, protecting, and educati[ng] their children, and therefore had "power" over their children. *Commentaries on the Laws of England* (1765).

Thus, in case after case, courts made clear that parents had a right to the child's labor and services until the child reached majority. . . . Relatedly, boys could not enlist in the military without parental consent. . . . Laws also set age limits restricting marriage without parental consent. . . . Indeed, the law imposed age limits on all manner of activities that required judgment and reason. Children could not vote, could not serve on juries, and generally could not be witnesses in criminal cases unless they were older than 14.

The history clearly shows a founding generation that believed parents to have complete authority over their minor children and expected parents to direct the development of those children. . . .

In light of this history, the Framers could not possibly have understood "the freedom of speech" to include an unqualified right to speak to minors. Specifically, I am sure that the founding generation would not have understood "the freedom of speech" to include a right to speak to children without going through their parents. As a consequence, I do not believe that laws limiting such speech—for example, by requiring parental consent to speak to a minor—"abridg[e] the freedom of speech" within the original meaning of the First Amendment. . . .

"The freedom of speech," as originally understood, does not include a right to speak to minors without going through the minors' parents or guardians. Therefore, I cannot agree that the statute at issue is facially unconstitutional under the First Amendment.

I respectfully dissent.

☐ *Justice BREYER, dissenting.*

Applying traditional First Amendment analysis, I would uphold the statute as constitutional on its face and would consequently reject the industries' facial challenge. . . .

The majority's claim that the California statute, if upheld, would create a "new categor[y] of unprotected speech" is overstated. No one here argues that depictions of violence, even extreme violence, *automatically* fall outside the First Amendment's protective scope as, for example, do obscenity and depictions of child pornography. We properly speak of *categories* of expression that lack protection when, like "child pornography," the category is broad, when it applies automatically, and when the State can prohibit everyone, including adults, from obtaining access to the material within it. But where, as here, careful analysis must precede a narrower judicial conclusion (say, denying protection to a shout of "fire" in a crowded theater, or to an effort to teach a terrorist group how to peacefully petition the United Nations), we do not normally describe the result as creating a "new category of unprotected speech." . . .

Video games combine action with expression. Were physical activity to predominate in a game, government could appropriately intervene, say by requiring parents to accompany children when playing a game involving actual target practice, or restricting the sale of toys presenting physical dangers to children. But because video games also embody important expressive and artistic elements, I agree with the Court that the First Amendment significantly limits the State's power to regulate. And I would determine whether the State has exceeded those limits by applying a strict standard of review. . . .

The interest that California advances in support of the statute is compelling. . . . As to the need to help parents guide their children, the Court noted in 1968 that "parental control or guidance cannot always be provided." Today, 5.3 million grade-school-age children of working parents are routinely home alone. Thus, it has, if anything, become more important to supplement parents' authority to guide their children's development.

As to the State's independent interest, we have pointed out that juveniles are more likely to show a "lack of maturity" and are "more vulnerable or susceptible to negative influences and outside pressures," and that their "character . . . is not as well formed as that of an adult." *Roper v. Simmons*, 543 U.S. 551 (2005). And we have therefore recognized "a compelling interest in protecting the physical and psychological well-being of minors."

At the same time, there is considerable evidence that California's statute significantly furthers this compelling interest. . . .

There are many scientific studies that support California's views. Social scientists, for example, have found *causal* evidence that playing these games results in harm. Longitudinal studies, which measure changes over time, have found that increased exposure to violent video games causes an increase in aggression over the same period.

Experimental studies in laboratories have found that subjects randomly assigned to play a violent video game subsequently displayed more characteristics of aggression than those who played nonviolent games.

Surveys of 8th and 9th grade students have found a correlation between playing violent video games and aggression.

And "meta-analysis," *i.e.*, studies of all the studies, have concluded that exposure to violent video games "was positively associated with aggressive behavior, aggressive cognition, and aggressive affect," and that "playing violent video games is a *causal* risk factor for long-term harmful outcomes."

The upshot is that California's statute, as applied to its heartland of applications (*i.e.*, buyers under 17; extremely violent, realistic video games), imposes a restriction on speech that is modest at most. That restriction is justified by a compelling interest (supplementing parents' efforts to prevent their children from purchasing potentially harmful violent, interactive material). And there is no equally effective, less restrictive alternative. California's statute is consequently constitutional on its face—though litigants remain free to challenge the statute as applied in particular instances, including any effort by the State to apply it to minors aged 17. . . .

This case is ultimately less about censorship than it is about education. Our Constitution cannot succeed in securing the liberties it seeks to protect unless we can raise future generations committed cooperatively to making our government work. Education, however, is about choices. Sometimes, children need to learn by making choices for themselves. Other times, choices are made for children—by their parents, by their teachers, and by the people acting democratically through their governments. In my view, the First Amendment does not disable government from helping parents make such a choice here—a choice not to have their children buy extremely violent, interactive video games, which they more than reasonably fear pose only the risk of harm to those children.

For these reasons, I respectfully dissent.

D | *Commercial Speech*

■ THE DEVELOPMENT OF LAW

Other Important Rulings on Commercial Speech and the First Amendment

CASE	VOTE	RULING
Sorrell v. IMS Health Inc., 131 S.Ct. 2653 (2011)	6:3	Writing for the Court, Justice Kennedy invalidated Vermont's Prescription Confidentiality Law

of 2007. That statute had restricted the disclosure and sale of pharmacy records that reveal the prescribing practices of individual doctors. Subject to certain exceptions, the information may not be disclosed by pharmacies for marketing purposes. The law was challenged by some pharmaceutical manufacturers and data-mining firms that collect such data and analyze it to produce reports on prescribers' behavior. Data miners lease these reports to pharmaceutical manufacturers, whose sales representatives use the reports to refine their marketing tactics and to increase sales. The majority held that, "Speech in aid of pharmaceutical marketing . . . is a form of expression protected by the Free Speech Clause of the First Amendment." That is because it is a content-based restriction aimed at particular speakers and cannot satisfy "heightened judicial scrutiny." In Justice Kennedy's words: "The Constitution 'does not enact Mr. Herbert Spencer's *Social Statics.*' *Lochner v. New York* (1905) (HOLMES, J., dissenting.) It does enact the First Amendment." Justices Breyer, Ginsburg, and Kagan dissented.

F | *Regulating the Broadcast and Cable Media, and the Internet*

The Court will revisit the Federal Communication Commission's (FCC) enforcement of its "indecency standard" in *FCC v. Fox Television Stations, Inc.* (No. 10-1293). In 2004, the FCC modified its indecency policy to include the broadcasting of "fleeting" expletives, punishable by fines. Fox and all other major broadcasting networks challenged the constitutionality of new policy. The Court of Appeals for the Second Circuit held that the policy change was arbitrary and capricious under the Administrative Procedures Act (APA) because the FCC did not provide adequate reasons for its change in policy. On appeal that decision was reversed by the Supreme Court, in *FCC v. Fox Television Stations,* 129 S.Ct. 1800 (2009), and remanded to the appellate court for consideration of the constitutionality of the policy change. On remand, the Second Circuit held that the FCC's policy was unconstitutional and impermissibly vague in failing to provide fair notice, because the networks were forced to choose between airing a program and risking a fine based on the policy or not airing the program at all. That choice, the appellate court concluded, had a "chilling effect" on First Amendment freedoms. The Supreme Court granted review of that decision and "whether the FCC's current indecency-enforcement regime violates the First or Fifth Amendment."

H | *Symbolic Speech and Speech-Plus-Conduct*

(2) *Speech-Plus-Conduct*

In a widely watched and emotional case, *Snyder v. Phelps* (2011) (excerpted below), the Court upheld First Amendment protection for picketers at military funerals in protest of tolerance for homosexuals, particularly in the military. Although reaffirming broad First Amendment protection for freedom of expression, the Court's opinion was notably narrowly tailored to the facts in the case.

Snyder v. Phelps
131 S.Ct. 1207 (2011)

Fred Phelps founded the Westboro Baptist Church, a small family-run church, in Topeka, Kansas, in 1955. The church preaches that God hates and punishes the United States for its tolerance of homosexuality, particularly in the military. During the last 20 years the church has publicized its message by picketing nearly 600 military funerals. One of those was for Marine Lance Corporal Matthew Snyder, who was killed in Iraq. Phelps read about Snyder's funeral and decided to travel to Maryland with six other Westboro Baptist parishioners to picket. The church notified authorities in advance of its intent and complied with police instructions in picketing, which took place within a 10- by 25-foot plot of public land adjacent to a public street, behind a temporary fence, approximately 1,000 feet from where the funeral was held. Several buildings also separated the picket site from the funeral and none of the picketers went into the cemetery.

Albert Snyder, the father of Matthew Snyder, objected and sued Phelps and the church for the tort of infliction of emotional distress, though he later testified that he could only see the tops of the picket signs as he drove to the funeral, he did not see what was written on the signs until later that night when watching a news broadcast covering the funeral. Phelps in turn countered that the demonstration was protected by the First Amendment.

A jury found for Snyder and awarded ten million dollars in damages, which a federal district court reduced to two million. On appeal, the Court of Appeals for the Fourth Circuit reversed and held that the picketing was First Amendment protected speech.

On appeal, the Supreme Court by an eight-to-one vote affirmed the appellate court. Chief Justice Roberts delivered the opinion for the Court, while Justice Breyer filed a concurrence, and Justice Alito filed a dissenting opinion.

☐ *CHIEF JUSTICE ROBERTS delivered the opinion of the Court.*

A jury held members of the Westboro Baptist Church liable for millions of dollars in damages for picketing near a soldier's funeral service. The picket signs reflected the church's view that the United States is overly tolerant of sin and that God kills American soldiers as punishment. The question presented is whether the First Amendment shields the church members from tort liability for their speech in this case.

Whether the First Amendment prohibits holding Westboro liable for its speech in this case turns largely on whether that speech is of public or private concern, as determined by all the circumstances of the case. "[S]peech on 'matters of public concern' . . . is 'at the heart of the First Amendment's protection.'" *Dun & Bradstreet, Inc. v. Greenmoss Builders, Inc.*, 472 U.S. 749 (1985). The First Amendment reflects "a profound national commitment to the principle that debate on public issues should be uninhibited, robust, and wide-open." *New York Times Co. v. Sullivan*, 376 U.S. 254 (1964). That is because "speech concerning public affairs is more than self-expression; it is the essence of self-government." *Garrison v. Louisiana*, 379 U.S. 64 (1964). Accordingly, "speech on public issues occupies the highest rung of the hierarchy of First Amendment values, and is entitled to special protection." *Connick v. Myers*, 461 U.S. 138 (1983).

Speech deals with matters of public concern when it can "be fairly considered as relating to any matter of political, social, or other concern to the community," *Connick*, or when it "is a subject of legitimate news interest; that is, a subject of general interest and of value and concern to the public." See *Cox Broadcasting Corp. v. Cohn*, 420 U.S. 469 (1975). The arguably "inappropriate or controversial character of a statement is irrelevant to the question whether it deals with a matter of public concern." *Rankin v. McPherson*, 483 U.S. 378 (1987).

Our opinion in *Dun & Bradstreet*, on the other hand, provides an example of speech of only private concern. In that case we held, as a general matter, that information about a particular individual's credit report "concerns no public issue." The content of the report, we explained, "was speech solely in the individual interest of the speaker and its specific business audience." That was confirmed by the fact that the particular report was sent to only five subscribers to the reporting service, who were bound not to disseminate it further.

Deciding whether speech is of public or private concern requires us to examine the "'content, form, and context'" of that speech, "'as revealed by the whole record.'" *Dun & Bradstreet*. The "content" of Westboro's signs plainly relates to broad issues of interest to society at large, rather than matters of "purely private concern." The placards read "God Hates the USA/Thank God for 9/11," "America is Doomed," "Don't Pray for the USA," "Thank

God for IEDs," "Fag Troops," "Semper Fi Fags," "God Hates Fags," "Maryland Taliban," "Fags Doom Nations," "Not Blessed Just Cursed," "Thank God for Dead Soldiers," "Pope in Hell," "Priests Rape Boys," "You're Going to Hell," and "God Hates You." While these messages may fall short of refined social or political commentary, the issues they highlight—the political and moral conduct of the United States and its citizens, the fate of our Nation, homosexuality in the military, and scandals involving the Catholic clergy—are matters of public import. The signs certainly convey Westboro's position on those issues, in a manner designed, unlike the private speech in *Dun & Bradstreet*, to reach as broad a public audience as possible. And even if a few of the signs—such as "You're Going to Hell" and "God Hates You"—were viewed as containing messages related to Matthew Snyder or the Snyders specifically, that would not change the fact that the overall thrust and dominant theme of Westboro's demonstration spoke to broader public issues.

Apart from the content of Westboro's signs, Snyder contends that the "context" of the speech—its connection with his son's funeral—makes the speech a matter of private rather than public concern. The fact that Westboro spoke in connection with a funeral, however, cannot by itself transform the nature of Westboro's speech. Westboro's signs, displayed on public land next to a public street, reflect the fact that the church finds much to condemn in modern society. Its speech is "fairly characterized as constituting speech on a matter of public concern," and the funeral setting does not alter that conclusion. . . .

Snyder goes on to argue that Westboro's speech should be afforded less than full First Amendment protection "not only because of the words" but also because the church members exploited the funeral "as a platform to bring their message to a broader audience." There is no doubt that Westboro chose to stage its picketing at the Naval Academy, the Maryland State House, and Matthew Snyder's funeral to increase publicity for its views and because of the relation between those sites and its views—in the case of the military funeral, because Westboro believes that God is killing American soldiers as punishment for the Nation's sinful policies.

Westboro's choice to convey its views in conjunction with Matthew Snyder's funeral made the expression of those views particularly hurtful to many, especially to Matthew's father. The record makes clear that the applicable legal term—"emotional distress"—fails to capture fully the anguish Westboro's choice added to Mr. Snyder's already incalculable grief. But Westboro conducted its picketing peacefully on matters of public concern at a public place adjacent to a public street. Such space occupies a "special position in terms of First Amendment protection." *United States v. Grace*, 461 U.S. 171 (1983). "[W]e have repeatedly referred to public streets as the archetype of a traditional public forum," noting that " '[t]ime out of mind' public streets and sidewalks have been used for public assembly and debate." *Frisby v. Schultz*, 487 U.S. 474 (1988). That said, "[e]ven protected speech is not equally permissible in all places and at all times." Westboro's choice of where and when to conduct its picketing is not beyond the Government's regulatory reach—it is "subject to reasonable time, place, or manner restrictions" that are consistent with the standards announced in this Court's precedents. *Clark v. Community for Creative Non-Violence*, 468 U.S. 288 (1984). Maryland now has a law imposing restrictions on funeral picketing, as do 43 other States and the Federal Government. To the extent these laws are content neutral, they raise very different questions from the tort verdict at issue in this case. Maryland's law, however, was not in effect at the time of the events at issue here, so we have no occasion to consider how it might apply to facts such as those before us, or whether it or other similar regulations are constitutional. . . .

Simply put, the church members had the right to be where they were. Westboro alerted local authorities to its funeral protest and fully complied with police guidance on where the picketing could be staged. The picketing was conducted under police supervision some 1,000 feet from the church, out of the sight of those at the church. The protest was not unruly; there was no shouting, profanity, or violence.

The record confirms that any distress occasioned by Westboro's picketing turned on the content and viewpoint of the message conveyed, rather than any interference with the funeral itself. A group of parishioners standing at the very spot where Westboro stood, holding signs that said "God Bless America" and "God Loves You," would not have been subjected to liability. It was what Westboro said that exposed it to tort damages.

Given that Westboro's speech was at a public place on a matter of public concern, that speech is entitled to "special protection" under the First Amendment. Such speech cannot be restricted simply because it is upsetting or arouses contempt. "If there is a bedrock principle underlying the First Amendment, it is that the government may not prohibit the expression of an idea simply because society finds the idea itself offensive or disagreeable." *Texas v. Johnson*, 491 U.S. 397 (1989). . . .

For all these reasons, the jury verdict imposing tort liability on Westboro for intentional infliction of emotional distress must be set aside.

The jury also found Westboro liable for the state law torts of intrusion upon seclusion and civil conspiracy. . . . Snyder argues that even assuming Westboro's speech is entitled to First Amendment protection generally, the church is not immunized from liability for intrusion upon seclusion because Snyder was a member of a captive audience at his son's funeral. We do not agree. In most circumstances, "the Constitution does not permit the government to decide which types of otherwise protected speech are sufficiently offensive to require protection for the unwilling listener or viewer. Rather, . . . the burden normally falls upon the viewer to avoid further bombardment of [his] sensibilities simply by averting [his] eyes." *Erznoznik v. Jacksonville*, 422 U.S. 205 (1975). As a result, "[t]he ability of government, consonant with the Constitution, to shut off discourse solely to protect others from hearing it is . . . dependent upon a showing that substantial privacy interests are being invaded in an essentially intolerable manner." *Cohen v. California*, 403 U.S. 15 (1971). . . .

Here, Westboro stayed well away from the memorial service. Snyder could see no more than the tops of the signs when driving to the funeral. And there is no indication that the picketing in any way interfered with the funeral service itself. We decline to expand the captive audience doctrine to the circumstances presented here. Because we find that the First Amendment bars Snyder from recovery for intentional infliction of emotional distress or intrusion upon seclusion—the alleged unlawful activity Westboro conspired to accomplish— we must likewise hold that Snyder cannot recover for civil conspiracy based on those torts.

Our holding today is narrow. We are required in First Amendment cases to carefully review the record, and the reach of our opinion here is limited by the particular facts before us. . . .

Speech is powerful. It can stir people to action, move them to tears of both joy and sorrow, and—as it did here—inflict great pain. On the facts before us, we cannot react to that pain by punishing the speaker. As a Nation we have chosen a different course—to protect even hurtful speech on public issues to ensure that we do not stifle public debate. That choice requires that we shield Westboro from tort liability for its picketing in this case.

□ *Justice BREYER, concurring.*

While I agree with the Court's conclusion that the picketing addressed matters of public concern, I do not believe that our First Amendment analysis can stop at that point. A State can sometimes regulate picketing, even picketing on matters of public concern. See *Frisby v. Schultz*, 487 U.S. 474 (1988).

Moreover, suppose that A were physically to assault B, knowing that the assault (being newsworthy) would provide A with an opportunity to transmit to the public his views on a matter of public concern. The constitutionally protected nature of the end would not shield A's use of unlawful, unprotected means. And in some circumstances the use of certain words as means would be similarly unprotected. See *Chaplinsky v. New Hampshire*, 315 U.S. 568 (1942) ("fighting words").

The dissent requires us to ask whether our holding unreasonably limits liability for intentional infliction of emotional distress—to the point where A (in order to draw attention to his views on a public matter) might launch a verbal assault upon B, a private person, publicly revealing the most intimate details of B's private life, while knowing that the revelation will cause B severe emotional harm. Does our decision leave the State powerless to protect the individual against invasions of, e.g., personal privacy, even in the most horrendous of such circumstances?

As I understand the Court's opinion, it does not hold or imply that the State is always powerless to provide private individuals with necessary protection. Rather, the Court has reviewed the underlying facts in detail, as will sometimes prove necessary where First Amendment values and state-protected (say, privacy-related) interests seriously conflict. That review makes clear that Westboro's means of communicating its views consisted of picketing in a place where picketing was lawful and in compliance with all police directions. The picketing could not be seen or heard from the funeral ceremony itself. And Snyder testified that he saw no more than the tops of the picketers' signs as he drove to the funeral. To uphold the application of state law in these circumstances would punish Westboro for seeking to communicate its views on matters of public concern without proportionately advancing the State's interest in protecting its citizens against severe emotional harm. Consequently, the First Amendment protects Westboro. As I read the Court's opinion, it holds no more.

□ *Justice ALITO, dissenting.*

Our profound national commitment to free and open debate is not a license for the vicious verbal assault that occurred in this case. . . .

Respondents and other members of their church have strong opinions on certain moral, religious, and political issues, and the First Amendment ensures that they have almost limitless opportunities to express their views. They may write and distribute books, articles, and other texts; they may create and disseminate video and audio recordings; they may circulate petitions; they may speak to individuals and groups in public forums and in any private venue that wishes to accommodate them; they may picket peacefully in countless locations; they may appear on television and speak on the radio; they may post messages on the Internet and send out e-mails. And they may express their views in terms that are "uninhibited," "vehement," and "caustic." *New York Times Co. v. Sullivan*, 376 U.S. 254 (1964).

It does not follow, however, that they may intentionally inflict severe emotional injury on private persons at a time of intense emotional sensitivity by launching vicious verbal attacks that make no contribution to public debate. To protect against such injury, "most if not all jurisdictions" permit recovery in tort for the intentional infliction of emotional distress (or IIED). *Hustler Magazine, Inc. v. Falwell*, 485 U.S. 46 (1988).

This is a very narrow tort with requirements that "are rigorous, and difficult to satisfy." To recover, a plaintiff must show that the conduct at issue caused harm that was truly severe.

A plaintiff must also establish that the defendant's conduct was "'so outrageous in character, and so extreme in degree, as to go beyond all possible bounds of decency, and to be regarded as atrocious, and utterly intolerable in a civilized community.'" . . .

This Court has recognized that words may "by their very utterance inflict injury" and that the First Amendment does not shield utterances that form "no essential part of any exposition of ideas, and are of such slight social value as a step to truth that any benefit that may be derived from them is clearly outweighed by the social interest in order and morality." *Chaplinsky v. New Hampshire*, 315 U.S. 568 (1942). When grave injury is intentionally inflicted by means of an attack like the one at issue here, the First Amendment should not interfere with recovery. . . .

In light of [the facts], it is abundantly clear that respondents, going far beyond commentary on matters of public concern, specifically attacked Matthew Snyder because (1) he was a Catholic and (2) he was a member of the United States military. Both Matthew and petitioner were private figures, and this attack was not speech on a matter of public concern. While commentary on the Catholic Church or the United States military constitutes speech on matters of public concern, speech regarding Matthew Snyder's purely private conduct does not. . . .

Respondents' outrageous conduct caused petitioner great injury, and the Court now compounds that injury by depriving petitioner of a judgment that acknowledges the wrong he suffered.

In order to have a society in which public issues can be openly and vigorously debated, it is not necessary to allow the brutalization of innocent victims like petitioner. I therefore respectfully dissent.

7

The Fourth Amendment Guarantee against Unreasonable Searches and Seizures

B | *Exceptions to the Fourth Amendment Warrant Requirement*

In its 2011–2012 term the Court will consider whether the Fourth Amendment was violated by the strip search of an individual who was arrested without an articulated reasonable suspicion that he possessed contraband or was dangerous, in *Florence v. Board of Chosen Freeholders* (Docket No. 10-945). A New Jersey state trooper had stopped a car in which Albert Florence was a passenger and arrested him on the basis of an outstanding warrant. Florence contested the validity of the warrant but was taken to the Burlington county jail, where he was subjected to a strip and body cavity search. He was held for six days, was transferred to another correctional facility, and underwent another strip search. The following day, the charges against him were dismissed. Subsequently, Florence sued, contending that his Fourth Amendment rights had been violated. A federal district court certified a class-action suit of individuals, including Florence, who had been subject to such strip searches, and certified the question of whether such suspicionless searches violate the Fourth Amendment. On appeal the Court of Appeals for the Third Circuit held that such strip searches are reasonable under the Fourth

Amendment based on a balancing test weighing the jails' security interests when taking in an inmate and the inmate's privacy interests.

In its 2011 term the Court will also consider whether the warrantless use of a tracking device on an individual's car in order to monitor its movements on public streets violates the Fourth Amendment, and whether the police violated the Fourth Amendment by installing the tracking device without a valid warrant or the consent of the owner. The case is *United States v. Jones* (No. 10-1259). In 2005, Jones and fellow co-conspirators were charged with conspiracy to distribute cocaine, among other charges. When investigating the alleged conspiracy, law enforcement agents obtained a warrant authorizing them to install and monitor a global positioning system (GPS) tracking device on Jones's car "within ten days of the issuance of the warrant and only within the District of Columbia." The agents, however, did not install the device until eleven days after the warrant was issued and they did so while the car was parked in a public parking lot in Maryland. At Jones's first trial, his co-defendants were acquitted on all but one count. The jury acquitted Jones on several counts but deadlocked on the conspiracy charge, resulting in a mistrial. In Jones's second trial, the prosecution filed a superseding indictment charging Jones with conspiracy to distribute five kilograms of cocaine and fifty grams of cocaine base. Jones's attorney moved to exclude the evidence because it was obtained through the use of a GPS tracking device. The trial court granted the motion in part, explaining that the data obtained from the GPA device while the car was on public roads was admissible but that obtained while the car was parked inside the garage was suppressed. On appeal, the Court of Appeals for the District of Columbia Circuit reversed, ruling that the 24-hour monitoring of the movements of the car during the course of several weeks constituted an impermissible search under the Fourth Amendment. The Supreme Court granted review of that decision and the issue of whether the warrantless placement and use of an electronic tracking device on Jones's car constituted an unreasonable search and seizure.

By an eight-to-one vote the Roberts Court expanded the "exigencies of the circumstances" exception to the requirement for a warrant for a search and seizure of property (see Vol. 2, Ch. 7) by approving a warrantless search and seizure based on "a police-created exigency" to justify a warrantless search because evidence might be destroyed so long as police do not "engag[e] or threaten[] to engage in conduct that violates the Fourth Amendment." In adopting that rule the Court rejected alternative tests, such as whether police acted in "bad faith" because that test turns on subjective motives. A test of "reasonable foreseeability" of the destruction of evidence was dismissed as too unpredictable, while drawing a line at whether police had time to obtain a warrant and didn't was deemed too restrictive. Under the new test, police could knock on a door and if they hear or see evidence being destroyed inside, their entry would be permissible. By contrast, police may not break down a door if the person inside won't open the door, since that violates the Fourth Amendment. Justice Alito delivered the opinion of the Court in *Kentucky v. King* (2011) (excerpted below), and Justice Ginsburg dissented.

Kentucky v. King
131 S.Ct. 1849 (2011)

Justice Alito in the opinion for the Court and Justice Ginsburg's dissent discuss the facts of the case and reach very different results. The Kentucky Supreme Court had held that evidence obtained in a warrantless search should be excluded because police could have obtained a warrant but instead conducted a warrantless search based on "a foreseeable exigency" of the possible destruction of contraband. That court's decision was reversed by an eight-to-one vote.

□ *Justice ALITO delivered the opinion of the Court.*

It is well established that "exigent circumstances," including the need to prevent the destruction of evidence, permit police officers to conduct an otherwise permissible search without first obtaining a warrant. In this case, we consider whether this rule applies when police, by knocking on the door of a residence and announcing their presence, cause the occupants to attempt to destroy evidence. The Kentucky Supreme Court held that the exigent circumstances rule does not apply in the case at hand because the police should have foreseen that their conduct would prompt the occupants to attempt to destroy evidence. We reject this interpretation of the exigent circumstances rule. The conduct of the police prior to their entry into the apartment was entirely lawful. They did not violate the Fourth Amendment or threaten to do so. In such a situation, the exigent circumstances rule applies.

This case concerns the search of an apartment in Lexington, Kentucky. Police officers set up a controlled buy of crack cocaine outside an apartment complex. Undercover Officer Gibbons watched the deal take place from an unmarked car in a nearby parking lot. After the deal occurred, Gibbons radioed uniformed officers to move in on the suspect. He told the officers that the suspect was moving quickly toward the breezeway of an apartment building, and he urged them to "hurry up and get there" before the suspect entered an apartment.

In response to the radio alert, the uniformed officers drove into the nearby parking lot, left their vehicles, and ran to the breezeway. Just as they entered the breezeway, they heard a door shut and detected a very strong odor of burnt marijuana. At the end of the breezeway, the officers saw two apartments, one on the left and one on the right, and they did not know which apartment the suspect had entered. Gibbons had radioed that the suspect was running into the apartment on the right, but the officers did not hear this statement because they had already left their vehicles. Because they smelled marijuana smoke emanating from the apartment on the left, they approached the door of that apartment.

Officer Steven Cobb, one of the uniformed officers who approached the door, testified that the officers banged on the left apartment door "as loud as [they] could" and announced, "'This is the police'" or "'Police, police, police.'" Cobb said that "[a]s soon as [the officers] started banging on the door," they "could hear people inside moving," and "[i]t sounded as [though] things were being moved inside the apartment." These noises, Cobb testified, led the officers to believe that drug-related evidence was about to be destroyed.

At that point, the officers announced that they "were going to make entry inside the apartment." Cobb then kicked in the door, the officers entered the apartment, and they found three people in the front room: respondent Hollis King, respondent's girlfriend, and a guest who was smoking marijuana. The officers performed a protective sweep of the apartment during which they saw marijuana and powder cocaine in plain view. In a subsequent search, they also discovered crack cocaine, cash, and drug paraphernalia.

Police eventually entered the apartment on the right. Inside, they found the suspected drug dealer who was the initial target of their investigation. [King was subsequently tried, convicted, and sentenced] to 11 years' imprisonment.

The Kentucky Court of Appeals affirmed. It held that exigent circumstances justified the warrantless entry because the police reasonably believed that evidence would be destroyed. The police did not impermissibly create the exigency, the court explained, because they did not deliberately evade the warrant requirement. The Supreme Court of Kentucky reversed. . . .

The text of the Amendment . . . expressly imposes two requirements. First, all searches and seizures must be reasonable. Second, a warrant may not be issued unless probable cause is properly established and the scope of the authorized search is set out with particularity. See *Payton v. New York*, 445 U.S. 573 (1980).

Although the text of the Fourth Amendment does not specify when a search warrant must be obtained, this Court has inferred that a warrant must generally be secured. "It is a 'basic principle of Fourth Amendment law,'" we have often said, "'that searches and seizures inside a home without a warrant are presumptively unreasonable.'" *Brigham City v. Stuart*, 547 U.S. 398 (2006). But we have also recognized that this presumption may be overcome in some circumstances because "[t]he ultimate touchstone of the Fourth Amendment is 'reasonableness.'" Accordingly, the warrant requirement is subject to certain reasonable exceptions.

One well-recognized exception applies when "'the exigencies of the situation' make the needs of law enforcement so compelling that [a] warrantless search is objectively reasonable under the Fourth Amendment." *Mincey v. Arizona*, 437 U.S. 385 (1978).

This Court has identified several exigencies that may justify a warrantless search of a home. Under the "emergency aid" exception, for example, "officers may enter a home without a warrant to render emergency assistance to an injured occupant or to protect an occupant from imminent injury." Police officers may enter premises without a warrant when they are in hot pursuit of a fleeing suspect. See *United States v. Santana*, 427 U.S. 38 (1976). And— what is relevant here—the need "to prevent the imminent destruction of evidence" has long been recognized as a sufficient justification for a warrantless search. *Brigham City*.

Over the years, lower courts have developed an exception to the exigent circumstances rule, the so-called "police-created exigency" doctrine. Under this doctrine, police may not rely on the need to prevent destruction of evidence when that exigency was "created" or "manufactured" by the conduct of the police.

In applying this exception for the "creation" or "manufacturing" of an exigency by the police, courts require something more than mere proof that fear of detection by the police caused the destruction of evidence. An additional showing is obviously needed because, as the Eighth Circuit has recognized, "in some sense the police always create the exigent circumstances." That is to say, in the vast majority of cases in which evidence is destroyed by persons who are engaged in illegal conduct, the reason for the destruction is fear that the evidence will fall into the hands of law enforcement. . . . Consequently, a rule that precludes the police from making a warrantless entry to prevent the destruction of evidence whenever their conduct causes the exigency would unreasonably shrink the reach of this well-established exception to the warrant requirement.

Presumably for the purpose of avoiding such a result, the lower courts have held that the police-created exigency doctrine requires more than simple causation, but the lower courts have not agreed on the test to be applied. Indeed, the petition in this case maintains that "[t]here are currently five different tests being used by the United States Courts of Appeals," and that some state courts have crafted additional tests.

Despite the welter of tests devised by the lower courts, the answer to the question presented in this case follows directly and clearly from the principle that permits warrantless searches in the first place. As previously noted, warrantless searches are allowed when the circumstances make it reasonable, within the meaning of the Fourth Amendment, to dispense with the warrant requirement. Therefore, the answer to the question before us is that the exigent circumstances rule justifies a warrantless search when the conduct of the police preceding the exigency is reasonable in the same sense. Where, as here, the police did not create the exigency by engaging or threatening to engage in conduct that violates the Fourth Amendment, warrantless entry to prevent the destruction of evidence is reasonable and thus allowed. . . .

Similarly, officers may seek consent-based encounters if they are lawfully present in the place where the consensual encounter occurs. See *INS v. Delgado*, 466 U.S. 210 (1984) (noting that officers who entered into consent-based encounters with employees in a factory building were "lawfully present [in the factory] pursuant to consent or a warrant"). If consent is freely given, it makes no difference that an officer may have approached the person with the hope or expectation of obtaining consent. . . .

The reasons for looking to objective factors, rather than subjective intent, are clear. Legal tests based on reasonableness are generally objective, and this Court has long taken the view that "evenhanded law enforcement is best achieved by the application of objective standards of conduct, rather than standards that depend upon the subjective state of mind of the officer." . . .

[W]e have rejected the notion that police may seize evidence without a warrant only when they come across the evidence by happenstance. In *Horton [v. California*, 496 U.S. 128 (1990)], we held that the police may seize evidence in plain view even though the officers may be "interested in an item of evidence and fully expec[t] to find it in the course of a search."

Adoption of a reasonable foreseeability test would also introduce an unacceptable degree of unpredictability. For example, whenever law enforcement officers knock on the door of premises occupied by a person who may be involved in the drug trade, there is some possibility that the occupants may possess drugs and may seek to destroy them. Under a reasonable foresee-ability test, it would be necessary to quantify the degree of predictability that must be reached before the police-created exigency doctrine comes into play. . . .

We have noted that "[t]he calculus of reasonableness must embody allow-ance for the fact that police officers are often forced to make split-second judgments—in circumstances that are tense, uncertain, and rapidly evolving." The reasonable foreseeability test would create unacceptable and unwarranted difficulties for law enforcement officers who must make quick decisions in the field, as well as for judges who would be required to determine after the fact whether the destruction of evidence in response to a knock on the door was reasonably foreseeable based on what the officers knew at the time. . . .

For these reasons, we conclude that the exigent circumstances rule ap-plies when the police do not gain entry to premises by means of an actual or threatened violation of the Fourth Amendment. This holding provides ample protection for the privacy rights that the Amendment protects.

When law enforcement officers who are not armed with a warrant knock on a door, they do no more than any private citizen might do. And whether the person who knocks on the door and requests the opportunity to speak is a police officer or a private citizen, the occupant has no obligation to open the door or to speak. When the police knock on a door but the occupants choose not to respond or to speak, "the investigation will have reached a conspicuously low point," and the occupants "will have the kind of warning that even the most elaborate security system cannot provide." And even if an occupant chooses to open the door and speak with the officers, the occupant need not allow the officers to enter the premises and may refuse to answer any questions at any time.

Occupants who choose not to stand on their constitutional rights but instead elect to attempt to destroy evidence have only themselves to blame for the warrantless exigent-circumstances search that may ensue. . . .

Like the court below, we assume for purposes of argument that an exi-gency existed. Because the officers in this case did not violate or threaten to violate the Fourth Amendment prior to the exigency, we hold that the exigency justified the warrantless search of the apartment.

The judgment of the Kentucky Supreme Court is reversed, and the case is remanded for further proceedings not inconsistent with this opinion.

☐ *Justice GINSBURG, dissenting*

The Court today arms the police with a way routinely to dishonor the Fourth Amendment's warrant requirement in drug cases. In lieu of presenting their evidence to a neutral magistrate, police officers may now knock, listen, then break the door down, never mind that they had ample time to obtain a warrant. I dissent from the Court's reduction of the Fourth Amendment's force.

The Fourth Amendment guarantees to the people "[t]he right . . . to be secure in their . . . houses . . . against unreasonable searches and seizures." Warrants to search, the Amendment further instructs, shall issue only upon a showing of "probable cause" to believe criminal activity is afoot. These complementary provisions are designed to ensure that police will seek the authorization of a neutral magistrate before undertaking a search or seizure. Exceptions to the warrant requirement, this Court has explained, must be "few in number and carefully delineated," if the main rule is to remain hardy. *United States v. United States Dist. Court for Eastern Dist. of Mich.*, 407 U.S. 297 (1972); see *Kyllo v. United States*, 533 U.S. 27 (2001).

This case involves a principal exception to the warrant requirement, the exception applicable in "exigent circumstances." "[C]arefully delineated," the exception should govern only in genuine emergency situations. Circumstances qualify as "exigent" when there is an imminent risk of death or serious injury, or danger that evidence will be immediately destroyed, or that a suspect will escape. The question presented: May police, who could pause to gain the approval of a neutral magistrate, dispense with the need to get a warrant by themselves creating exigent circumstances? I would answer no, as did the Kentucky Supreme Court. The urgency must exist, I would rule, when the police come on the scene, not subsequent to their arrival, prompted by their own conduct.

Two pillars of our Fourth Amendment jurisprudence should have controlled the Court's ruling: First, "whenever practical, [the police must] obtain advance judicial approval of searches and seizures through the warrant procedure," *Terry v. Ohio*, 392 U.S. 1 (1968); second, unwarranted "searches and seizures inside a home" bear heightened scrutiny, *Payton v. New York*, 445 U.S. 573 (1980). The warrant requirement, Justice JACKSON observed, ranks among the "fundamental distinctions between our form of government, where officers are under the law, and the police-state where they are the law." *Johnson v. United States*, 333 U.S. 10 (1948). The Court has accordingly declared warrantless searches, in the main, " per se unreasonable." *Mincey v. Arizona*, 437 U.S. 385 (1978). "[T]he police bear a heavy burden," the Court has cautioned, "when attempting to demonstrate an urgent need that might justify warrantless searches." *Welsh v. Wisconsin*, 466 U.S. 740 (1984).

That heavy burden has not been carried here. There was little risk that drug-related evidence would have been destroyed had the police delayed the search pending a magistrate's authorization. As the Court recognizes, "[p]ersons in possession of valuable drugs are unlikely to destroy them unless they fear discovery by the police." Nothing in the record shows that, prior to the knock at the apartment door, the occupants were apprehensive about police proximity. . . .

As above noted, to justify the police activity in this case, Kentucky invoked the once-guarded exception for emergencies "in which the delay necessary to obtain a warrant . . . threaten[s] 'the destruction of evidence.'" *Schmerber v. California*, 384 U.S. 757 (1966). To fit within this exception, "police action literally must be [taken] 'now or never' to preserve the evidence of the crime." *Roaden v. Kentucky*, 413 U.S. 496 (1973).

The existence of a genuine emergency depends not only on the state of necessity at the time of the warrantless search; it depends, first and foremost, on "actions taken by the police preceding the warrantless search."

Under an appropriately reined-in "emergency" or "exigent circumstances" exception, the result in this case should not be in doubt. The target of the investigation's entry into the building, and the smell of marijuana seeping under the apartment door into the hallway, the Kentucky Supreme Court rightly determined, gave the police "probable cause . . . sufficient . . . to obtain a warrant to search the . . . apartment." As that court observed, nothing made it impracticable for the police to post officers on the premises while proceeding to obtain a warrant authorizing their entry.

In *Johnson*, the Court confronted this scenario: standing outside a hotel room, the police smelled burning opium and heard "some shuffling or noise" coming from the room. Could the police enter the room without a warrant? The Court answered no. Explaining why, the Court said: "The right of officers to thrust themselves into a home is . . . a grave concern, not only to the individual but to a society which chooses to dwell in reasonable security and freedom from surveillance. When the right of privacy must reasonably yield to the right of search is, as a rule, to be decided by a judicial officer, not a policeman . . . .

"If the officers in this case were excused from the constitutional duty of presenting their evidence to a magistrate, it is difficult to think of [any] case in which [a warrant] should be required." I agree, and would not allow an expedient knock to override the warrant requirement. Instead, I would accord that core requirement of the Fourth Amendment full respect. When possible, "a warrant must generally be secured," the Court acknowledges. There is every reason to conclude that securing a warrant was entirely feasible in this case, and no reason to contract the Fourth Amendment's dominion.

F | *The Exclusionary Rule*

A solid majority of the Roberts Court held that warrantless searches of cars incident to an arrest of occupants made with reasonable reliance on binding precedents do not trigger the exclusionary rule, even if the kind of search conducted is later found to violate the Fourth Amendment. Writing for the Court in *Davis v. United States* (2011) (excerpted below), Justice Alito's opinion swept broadly with regard to "good faith" exceptions to the exclusionary rule and with respect to the retroactivity to pending cases of new rulings on impermissible searches and seizures. Notably, the majority expressly held that the exclusionary rule is merely a judicially created remedy and not a principle commanded by the Fourth Amendment. Justices Ginsburg and Breyer dissented.

Davis v. United States
131 S.Ct. 2419 (2011)

In Greenville, Alabama, Willie Davis was arrested by police during a routine vehicle stop for giving a false name. The police searched the car and found a revolver. Davis was arrested, tried and convicted for being a felon in possession of a firearm. At trial, his attorney moved to exclude the evidence, even though he knew that it complied with existing precedents. While Davis's appeal was pending, the Supreme Court announced a new rule on automobile searches incident to arrests of occupants, in *Arizona v. Gant*, 129 S.Ct. 1710 (2009). A panel of the Court of Appeals for the Eleventh Circuit held that, under *Gant*, the vehicle search in his case violated the Fourth Amendment but declined to suppress the evidence and affirmed Davis's conviction. That decision was appealed and granted review.

The appellate court's decision was affirmed by a seven-to-two vote. Justice Alito delivered the opinion for the Court. Justice Sotomayor filed a concurring opinion. Justice Breyer filed a dissenting opinion, which Justice Ginsburg joined.

□ *JUSTICE ALITO delivered the opinion of the Court.*

The question here is whether to apply [the exclusionary rule] when the police conduct a search in compliance with binding precedent that is later overruled. Because suppression would do nothing to deter police misconduct in these circumstances, and because it would come at a high cost to both the truth and the public safety, we hold that searches conducted in objectively reasonable reliance on binding appellate precedent are not subject to the exclusionary rule.

The question presented arises in this case as a result of a shift in our Fourth Amendment jurisprudence on searches of automobiles incident to arrests of recent occupants.

Under this Court's decision in *Chimel v. California*, 395 U.S. 752 (1969), a police officer who makes a lawful arrest may conduct a warrantless search of the arrestee's person and the area "within his immediate control." This rule "may be stated clearly enough," but in the early going after *Chimel* it proved difficult to apply, particularly in cases that involved searches "inside [of] automobile[s] after the arrestees [we]re no longer in [them]." See *New York v. Belton*, 453 U.S. 454 (1981). . . .

In *Belton*, a police officer conducting a traffic stop lawfully arrested four occupants of a vehicle and ordered the arrestees to line up, un-handcuffed, along the side of the thruway. The officer then searched the vehicle's passenger compartment and found cocaine inside a jacket that lay on the backseat. This Court upheld the search as reasonable incident to the occupants' arrests. In an opinion that repeatedly stressed the need for a "straightforward," "workable rule" to guide police conduct, the Court announced "that when a policeman has made a lawful custodial arrest of the occupant of an automobile, he may, as a contemporaneous incident of that arrest, search the passenger compartment of that automobile."

For years, *Belton* was widely understood to have set down a simple, bright-line rule. . . .

Not every court, however, agreed with this reading of *Belton*. In *State v. Gant*, the Arizona Supreme Court considered an automobile search conducted after the vehicle's occupant had been arrested, handcuffed, and locked in a patrol car. The court distinguished *Belton* as a case in which "four unsecured" arrestees "presented an immediate risk of loss of evidence and an obvious threat to [a] lone officer's safety." The court held that where no such "exigencies exis[t]"—where the arrestee has been subdued and the scene secured—the rule of *Belton* does not apply.

This Court granted *certiorari* in *Gant* and affirmed in a 5-to-4 decision. *Arizona v. Gant*, [129 S.Ct. 1710] (2009). Four of the Justices in the majority agreed with the Arizona Supreme Court that *Belton's* holding applies only where "the arrestee is unsecured and within reaching distance of the passenger compartment at the time of the search." The four dissenting Justices, by contrast, understood *Belton* to have explicitly adopted the simple, bright-line rule stated in the *Belton* Court's opinion. Justice SCALIA, who provided the fifth vote to affirm in *Gant*, agreed with the dissenters' understanding of *Belton's* holding. Justice SCALIA favored a more explicit and complete overruling of *Belton*, but he joined what became the majority opinion to avoid "a 4-to-1-to-4" disposition. As a result, the Court adopted a new, two-part rule under which an automobile search incident to a recent occupant's arrest is constitutional (1) if the arrestee is within reaching distance of the vehicle during the search, or (2) if the police have reason to believe that the vehicle contains "evidence relevant to the crime of arrest."

The search at issue in this case took place a full two years before this Court announced its new rule in *Gant*. . . .

The Fourth Amendment protects the "right of the people to be secure in their persons, houses, papers, and effects, against unreasonable searches and seizures." The Amendment says nothing about suppressing evidence obtained in violation of this command. That rule—the exclusionary rule—is a "prudential" doctrine, *Pennsylvania Bd. of Probation and Parole v. Scott*, 524 U.S. 357 (1998), created by this Court to "compel respect for the constitutional guaranty." *Elkins v. United States*, 364 U.S. 206 (1960); see *Weeks v. United States*, 232 U.S. 383 (1914); *Mapp v. Ohio*, 367 U.S. 643 (1961). Exclusion is "not a personal constitutional right," nor is it designed to "redress the injury" occasioned by an unconstitutional search. *Stone v. Powell*, 428 U.S. 465 (1976).

Real deterrent value is a "necessary condition for exclusion," but it is not "a sufficient" one. The analysis must also account for the "substantial social costs" generated by the rule. Exclusion exacts a heavy toll on both the judicial system and society at large. It almost always requires courts to ignore reliable, trustworthy evidence bearing on guilt or innocence. And its bottom-line effect, in many cases, is to suppress the truth and set the criminal loose in the community without punishment. Our cases hold that society must swallow this bitter pill when necessary, but only as a "last resort." . . .

In time, however, we came to acknowledge the exclusionary rule for what it undoubtedly is—a "judicially created remedy" of this Court's own making. We abandoned the old, "reflexive" application of the doctrine, and imposed a more rigorous weighing of its costs and deterrence benefits. In a line of cases beginning with *United States v. Leon*, 468 U.S. 897 [(1984)], we also recalibrated our cost-benefit analysis in exclusion cases to focus the inquiry on the "flagrancy of the police misconduct" at issue.

The basic insight of the *Leon* line of cases is that the deterrence benefits of exclusion "var[y] with the culpability of the law enforcement conduct" at issue. When the police exhibit "deliberate," "reckless," or "grossly negligent" disregard for Fourth Amendment rights, the deterrent value of exclusion is strong and tends to outweigh the resulting costs. But when the police act with an objectively "reasonable good-faith belief" that their conduct is lawful, or when their conduct involves only simple, "isolated" negligence, the "'deterrence rationale loses much of its force,'" and exclusion cannot "pay its way."

The Court has over time applied this "good-faith" exception across a range of cases. *Leon* itself, for example, held that the exclusionary rule does not apply when the police conduct a search in "objectively reasonable reliance" on a warrant later held invalid. . . .

The question in this case is whether to apply the exclusionary rule when the police conduct a search in objectively reasonable reliance on binding judicial precedent. At the time of the search at issue here, we had not yet decided *Arizona v. Gant* and the Eleventh Circuit had interpreted our decision in *New York v. Belton*, 453 U.S. 454 [(1981)], to establish a bright-line rule authorizing the search of a vehicle's passenger compartment incident to a recent occupant's arrest. . . .

Under our exclusionary-rule precedents, this acknowledged absence of police culpability dooms Davis's claim. Police practices trigger the harsh sanction of exclusion only when they are deliberate enough to yield "meaningfu[l]" deterrence, and culpable enough to be "worth the price paid by the justice system." The conduct of the officers here was neither of these things. The officers who conducted the search did not violate Davis's Fourth Amendment rights deliberately, recklessly, or with gross negligence. Nor does this case involve any "recurring or systemic negligence" on the part of law enforcement. The police acted in strict compliance with binding precedent, and their behavior was not wrongful. Unless the exclusionary rule is to become a strict-liability regime, it can have no application in this case.

Indeed, in 27 years of practice under *Leon*'s good-faith exception, we have "never applied" the exclusionary rule to suppress evidence obtained as a result of nonculpable, innocent police conduct. . . .

The principal argument of both the dissent and Davis is that the exclusionary rule's availability to enforce new Fourth Amendment precedent is a retroactivity issue, see *Griffith v. Kentucky*, 479 U.S. 314 (1987), not a good-faith issue. They contend that applying the good-faith exception where police have relied on overruled precedent effectively revives the discarded retroactivity regime of *Linkletter v. Walker*, 381 U.S. 618 (1965).

In *Linkletter*, we held that the retroactive effect of a new constitutional rule of criminal procedure should be determined on a case-by-case weighing of interests. For each new rule, *Linkletter* required courts to consider a three-factor balancing test that looked to the "purpose" of the new rule, "reliance" on the old rule by law enforcement and others, and the effect retroactivity would have "on the administration of justice." . . . In *Linkletter* itself, the balance of interests prompted this Court to conclude that *Mapp v. Ohio*, 367 U.S. 643 [(1961)]—which incorporated the exclusionary rule against the States—should not apply retroactively to cases already final on direct review.

Over time, *Linkletter* proved difficult to apply in a consistent, coherent way. Individual applications of the standard "produced strikingly divergent results" that many saw as "incompatible" and "inconsistent." . . . Eventually, and after more than 20 years of toil under *Linkletter*, the Court adopted Justice HARLAN's view and held that newly announced rules of constitutional criminal procedure must apply "retroactively to all cases, state or federal, pending on direct review or not yet final, with no exception." *Griffith [v. Kentucky*, 479 U.S. 314 (1987)].

The dissent and Davis argue that applying the good-faith exception in this case is "incompatible" with our retroactivity precedent under *Griffith*. We think this argument conflates what are two distinct doctrines.

Our retroactivity jurisprudence is concerned with whether, as a categorical matter, a new rule is available on direct review as a potential ground for relief. Retroactive application under *Griffith* lifts what would otherwise be a categorical bar to obtaining redress for the government's violation of a newly announced constitutional rule. . . .

When this Court announced its decision in *Gant*, Davis's conviction had not yet become final on direct review. *Gant* therefore applies retroactively to this case. Davis may invoke its newly announced rule of substantive Fourth Amendment law as a basis for seeking relief. The question, then, becomes one of remedy, and on that issue Davis seeks application of the exclusionary rule. But exclusion of evidence does not automatically follow from the fact that a Fourth Amendment violation occurred. The remedy is subject to exceptions and applies only where its "purpose is effectively advanced." . . .

It is true that, under the old retroactivity regime of *Linkletter*, the Court's decisions on the "retroactivity problem in the context of the exclusionary rule" did take into account whether "law enforcement officers reasonably believed in good faith" that their conduct was in compliance with governing law. As a matter of retroactivity analysis, that approach is no longer applicable. It does not follow, however, that reliance on binding precedent is irrelevant in applying the good-faith exception to the exclusionary rule. . . . That reasonable reliance by police was once a factor in our retroactivity cases does not make it any less relevant under our *Leon* line of cases.

Davis also contends that applying the good-faith exception to searches conducted in reliance on binding precedent will stunt the development of Fourth Amendment law. With no possibility of suppression, criminal defendants will have no incentive, Davis maintains, to request that courts overrule precedent.

This argument is difficult to reconcile with our modern understanding of the role of the exclusionary rule. We have never held that facilitating the overruling of precedent is a relevant consideration in an exclusionary-rule case. Rather, we have said time and again that the sole purpose of the exclusionary rule is to deter misconduct by law enforcement. . . .

It is one thing for the criminal "to go free because the constable has blundered." *People v. Defore*, 242 N.Y. 13 (1926) (CARDOZO, J.). It is quite another to set the criminal free because the constable has scrupulously adhered to governing law. Excluding evidence in such cases deters no police misconduct and imposes substantial social costs. We therefore hold that when the police conduct a search in objectively reasonable reliance on binding appellate precedent, the exclusionary rule does not apply.

☐ *Justice BREYER, with whom Justice GINSBURG joins, dissenting.*

In 2009, in *Arizona v. Gant*, this Court held that a police search of an automobile without a warrant violates the Fourth Amendment if the police have previously removed the automobile's occupants and placed them securely in a squad car. The present case involves these same circumstances, and it was pending on appeal when this Court decided *Gant*. Because *Gant* represents a "shift" in the Court's Fourth Amendment jurisprudence, we must decide whether and how *Gant's* new rule applies here.

I agree with the Court about whether *Gant's* new rule applies. It does apply. Between 1965, when the Court decided *Linkletter v. Walker* and 1987, when it decided *Griffith v. Kentucky*, that conclusion would have been more difficult to reach. Under *Linkletter*, the Court determined a new rule's retroactivity by looking to several different factors, including whether the new rule represented a "clear break" with the past and the degree of "reliance by law enforcement authorities on the old standards." And the Court would often not apply the new rule to identical cases still pending on appeal.

After 22 years of struggling with its *Linkletter* approach, however, the Court decided in *Griffith* that *Linkletter* had proved unfair and unworkable. It then substituted a clearer approach, stating that "a new rule for the conduct of criminal prosecutions is to be applied retroactively to all cases, state or federal, pending on direct review or not yet final, with no exception for cases in which the new rule constitutes a 'clear break' with the past." The Court today, following *Griffith*, concludes that *Gant* s new rule applies here. And to that extent I agree with its decision.

The Court goes on, however, to decide how *Gant's* new rule will apply. And here it adds a fatal twist. While conceding that, like the search in *Gant*, this search violated the Fourth Amendment , it holds that, unlike *Gant*, this defendant is not entitled to a remedy. That is because the Court finds a new "good faith" exception which prevents application of the normal remedy for a Fourth Amendment violation, namely, suppression of the illegally seized evidence. Leaving Davis with a right but not a remedy, the Court "keep[s] the word of promise to our ear" but "break[s] it to our hope."

At this point I can no longer agree with the Court. A new "good faith" exception and this Court's retroactivity decisions are incompatible. For one thing, the Court's distinction between (1) retroactive application of a new rule and (2) availability of a remedy is highly artificial and runs counter to precedent. To determine that a new rule is retroactive is to determine that, at least in the normal case, there is a remedy. As we have previously said, the "source of a 'new rule' is the Constitution itself, not any judicial power to create new rules of law"; hence, "[w]hat we are actually determining when we assess the 'retroactivity' of a new rule is not the temporal scope of a newly announced right, but whether a violation of the right that occurred prior to the announcement of the new rule will entitle a criminal defendant to the relief sought." The Court's "good faith" exception (unlike, say, inevitable discovery, a remedial doctrine that applies only upon occasion) creates "a categorical bar to obtaining redress" in every case pending when a precedent is overturned.

For another thing, the Court's holding re-creates the very problems that led the Court to abandon *Linkletter's* approach to retroactivity in favor of *Griffith's*. One such problem concerns workability. The Court says that its exception applies where there is "objectively reasonable" police "reliance on binding appellate precedent." But to apply the term "binding appellate precedent" often requires resolution of complex questions of degree. . . .

At the same time, Fourth Amendment precedents frequently require courts to "slosh" their "way through the fact bound morass of 'reasonableness.'" Suppose an officer's conduct is consistent with the language of a Fourth Amendment rule that a court of appeals announced in a case with clearly distinguishable facts? Suppose the case creating the relevant precedent did not directly announce any general rule but involved highly analogous facts? What about a rule that all other jurisdictions, but not the defendant's jurisdiction, had previously accepted? What rules can be developed for determining when, where, and how these different kinds of precedents do, or do not, count as relevant "binding precedent"? The *Linkletter*-like result is likely complex legal argument and police force confusion.

Another such problem concerns fairness. Today's holding, like that in *Linkletter*, "violates basic norms of constitutional adjudication." It treats the defendant in a case announcing a new rule one way while treating similarly situated defendants whose cases are pending on appeal in a different way. . . .

Perhaps more important, the Court's rationale for creating its new "good faith" exception threatens to undermine well-settled Fourth Amendment law. The Court correctly says that pre-*Gant* Eleventh Circuit precedent had held that a *Gant*-type search was constitutional; hence the police conduct in this case, consistent with that precedent, was "innocent." But the Court then finds this fact sufficient to create a new "good faith" exception to the exclusionary rule. It reasons that the "sole purpose" of the exclusionary rule "is to deter future Fourth Amendment violations." The "deterrence benefits of exclusion vary with the culpability of the law enforcement conduct at issue." Those benefits are sufficient to justify exclusion where "police exhibit deliberate, reckless, or grossly negligent disregard for Fourth Amendment rights." But those benefits do not justify exclusion where, as here, the police act with "simple, isolated negligence" or an "objectively reasonable good-faith belief that their conduct is lawful."

If the Court means what it says, what will happen to the exclusionary rule, a rule that the Court adopted nearly a century ago for federal courts, *Weeks v. United States* and made applicable to state courts a half century ago through the Fourteenth Amendment, *Mapp v. Ohio*? The Court has thought of that rule not as punishment for the individual officer or as reparation for the individual defendant but more generally as an effective way to secure enforcement of the Fourth Amendment's commands. This Court has deviated from the "suppression" norm in the name of "good faith" only a handful of times and in limited, atypical circumstances: where a magistrate has erroneously issued a warrant, *United States v. Leon*, 468 U.S. 897 (1984); where a database has erroneously informed police that they have a warrant, *Arizona v. Evans*, 514 U.S. 1 (1995), *Herring v. United States*, 555 U.S. 135 (2009); and where an unconstitutional statute purported to authorize the search, *Illinois v. Krull*, 480 U.S. 340 (1987).

The fact that such exceptions are few and far between is understandable. Defendants frequently move to suppress evidence on Fourth Amendment grounds. In many, perhaps most, of these instances the police, uncertain of how the Fourth Amendment applied to the particular factual circumstances they faced, will have acted in objective good faith. Yet, in a significant percentage of these instances, courts will find that the police were wrong. And, unless the police conduct falls into one of the exceptions previously noted, courts have required the suppression of the evidence seized. . . .

In sum, I fear that the Court's opinion will undermine the exclusionary rule. And I believe that the Court wrongly departs from *Griffith* regardless. Instead I would follow *Griffith*, apply *Gant*'s rule retroactively to this case, and require suppression of the evidence. Such an approach is consistent with our precedent, and it would indeed affect no more than "an exceedingly small set of cases."

For these reasons, with respect, I dissent.

8

THE FIFTH AMENDMENT GUARANTEE AGAINST SELF-ACCUSATION

A | Coerced Confessions and Police Interrogations

In its 2010–2011 term a bare majority of the Court held that in determining whether minors are in "police custody," for the purposes of triggering the requirement of giving *Miranda* warnings of the right to remain silent, their age may be taken into consideration, in *J. D. B. v. North Carolina* (excerpted below). At issue was the police questioning and the confession of a thirteen-year-old at school. Justice Alito, joined by Chief Justice Roberts and Justices Scalia and Thomas, dissented, contending that the majority was departing from *Miranda*'s "bright-line rule" on when an individual becomes a "suspect" and reverting to the older "totality of circumstances" rule for determining coerced confessions.

J. D. B. v. North Carolina
131 S.Ct. 2394 (2011)

Justice Sotomayor discusses the facts in this case in her opinion for the Court. Justice Alito filed a dissenting opinion, joined by Chief Justice Roberts and Justices Scalia and Thomas.

☐ *Justice SOTOMAYOR delivered the opinion of the Court.*

This case presents the question whether the age of a child subjected to police questioning is relevant to the custody analysis of *Miranda v. Arizona*, 384 U.S. 436 (1966). It is beyond dispute that children will often feel bound to submit to police questioning when an adult in the same circumstances would feel free to leave. Seeing no reason for police officers or courts to blind themselves to that commonsense reality, we hold that a child's age properly informs the *Miranda* custody analysis.

Petitioner J. D. B. was a 13-year-old, seventh-grade student attending class at Smith Middle School in Chapel Hill, North Carolina when he was removed from his classroom by a uniformed police officer, escorted to a closed-door conference room, and questioned by police for at least half an hour.

This was the second time that police questioned J. D. B. in the span of a week. Five days earlier, two home break-ins occurred, and various items were stolen. Police stopped and questioned J. D. B. after he was seen behind a residence in the neighborhood where the crimes occurred. That same day, police also spoke to J. D. B.'s grandmother—his legal guardian—as well as his aunt.

Police later learned that a digital camera matching the description of one of the stolen items had been found at J. D. B.'s middle school and seen in J. D. B.'s possession. Investigator DiCostanzo, the juvenile investigator with the local police force who had been assigned to the case, went to the school to question J. D. B. Upon arrival, DiCostanzo informed the uniformed police officer on detail to the school (a so-called school resource officer), the assistant principal, and an administrative intern that he was there to question J. D. B. about the break-ins. . . .

Questioning began with small talk—discussion of sports and J. D. B.'s family life. DiCostanzo asked, and J. D. B. agreed, to discuss the events of the prior weekend. Denying any wrongdoing, J. D. B. explained that he had been in the neighborhood where the crimes occurred because he was seeking work mowing lawns. DiCostanzo pressed J. D. B. for additional detail about his efforts to obtain work; asked J. D. B. to explain a prior incident, when one of the victims returned home to find J. D. B. behind her house; and confronted J. D. B. with the stolen camera. The assistant principal urged J. D. B. to "do the right thing," warning J. D. B. that "the truth always comes out in the end."

Eventually, J. D. B. asked whether he would "still be in trouble" if he returned the "stuff." In response, DiCostanzo explained that return of the stolen items would be helpful, but "this thing is going to court" regardless. DiCostanzo then warned that he may need to seek a secure custody order if he believed that J. D. B. would continue to break into other homes. When J. D. B. asked what a secure custody order was, DiCostanzo explained that "it's where you get sent to juvenile detention before court."

After learning of the prospect of juvenile detention, J. D. B. confessed that he and a friend were responsible for the break-ins. DiCostanzo only then informed J. D. B. that he could refuse to answer the investigator's questions and that he was free to leave. Asked whether he understood, J. D. B. nodded and provided further detail, including information about the location of the stolen items. Eventually J. D. B. wrote a statement, at DiCostanzo's request. When the bell rang indicating the end of the school day, J. D. B. was allowed to leave to catch the bus home.

Two juvenile petitions were filed against J. D. B., each alleging one count of breaking and entering and one count of larceny. J. D. B.'s public defender moved to suppress his statements and the evidence derived therefrom, arguing that suppression was necessary because J. D. B. had been "interrogated by police in a custodial setting without being afforded *Miranda* warning[s]," and because his statements were involuntary under the totality of the circumstances test. After a suppression hearing at which DiCostanzo and J. D. B. testified, the trial court denied the motion, deciding that J. D. B. was not in custody at the time of the schoolhouse interrogation and that his statements were voluntary. As a result, J. D. B. entered a transcript of admission to all four counts, renewing his objection to the denial of his motion to suppress, and the court adjudicated J. D. B. delinquent.

A divided panel of the North Carolina Court of Appeals affirmed. The North Carolina Supreme Court held, over two dissents, that J. D. B. was not in custody when he confessed, "declin[ing] to extend the test for custody to include consideration of the age . . . of an individual subjected to questioning by police."

We granted *certiorari* to determine whether the *Miranda* custody analysis includes consideration of a juvenile suspect's age.

Any police interview of an individual suspected of a crime has "coercive aspects to it." *Oregon v. Mathiason*, 429 U.S. 492 (1977). Only those interrogations that occur while a suspect is in police custody, however, "heighte[n] the risk" that statements obtained are not the product of the suspect's free choice. *Dickerson v. United States*, 530 U.S. 428 (2000).

By its very nature, custodial police interrogation entails "inherently compelling pressures." *Miranda*. Even for an adult, the physical and psychological isolation of custodial interrogation can "undermine the individual's will to resist and . . . compel him to speak where he would not otherwise do so freely." Indeed, the pressure of custodial interrogation is so immense that it "can induce a frighteningly high percentage of people to confess to crimes they never committed." That risk is all the more troubling—and recent studies suggest, all the more acute—when the subject of custodial interrogation is a juvenile.

Recognizing that the inherently coercive nature of custodial interrogation "blurs the line between voluntary and involuntary statements," *Dickerson*, this Court in *Miranda* adopted a set of prophylactic measures designed to safeguard the constitutional guarantee against self-incrimination. Prior to questioning, a suspect "must be warned that he has a right to remain silent, that any statement he does make may be used as evidence against him, and that he has a right to the presence of an attorney, either retained or appointed." And, if a suspect makes a statement during custodial interrogation, the burden is on the Government to show, as a "prerequisit[e]" to the statement's admissibility as evidence in the Government's case in chief, that the defendant "voluntarily, knowingly and intelligently" waived his rights.

Because these measures protect the individual against the coercive nature of custodial interrogation, they are required "only where there has been such a restriction on a person's freedom as to render him 'in custody.'" *Stansbury v. California*, 511 U.S. 318 (1994). As we have repeatedly emphasized, whether a suspect is "in custody" is an objective inquiry. "Two discrete inquiries are essential to the determination: first, what were the circumstances surrounding the interrogation; and second, given those circumstances, would a reasonable person have felt he or she was at liberty to terminate the interrogation and leave. Once the scene is set and the players' lines and actions are reconstructed, the court must apply an objective test to resolve the ultimate inquiry: was there a formal arrest or restraint on freedom of movement of the degree associated with formal arrest." *Thompson v. Keohane*, 516 U.S. 99 (1995). Rather than demarcate a limited set of relevant circumstances, we have required police officers and courts to "examine all of the circumstances surrounding the interrogation," including any circumstance that "would have affected how a reasonable person" in the suspect's position "would perceive his or her freedom to leave." On the other hand, the "subjective views harbored by either the interrogating officers or the person being questioned" are irrelevant. The test, in other words, involves no consideration of the "actual mindset" of the particular suspect subjected to police questioning.

The benefit of the objective custody analysis is that it is "designed to give clear guidance to the police." Police must make in-the-moment judgments as to when to administer *Miranda* warnings. By limiting analysis to the objective circumstances of the interrogation, and asking how a reasonable person in the suspect's position would understand his freedom to terminate questioning and leave, the objective test avoids burdening police with the task of anticipating the idiosyncrasies of every individual suspect and divining how those particular traits affect each person's subjective state of mind.

The State and its *amici* contend that a child's age has no place in the custody analysis, no matter how young the child subjected to police questioning. We cannot agree. In some circumstances, a child's age "would have affected how a reasonable person" in the suspect's position "would perceive his or her freedom to leave." That is, a reasonable child subjected to police questioning will sometimes feel pressured to submit when a reasonable adult would feel free to go. We think it clear that courts can account for that reality without doing any damage to the objective nature of the custody analysis. . . .

Time and again, this Court has drawn these commonsense conclusions for itself. We have observed that children "generally are less mature and responsible than adults;" that they "often lack the experience, perspective, and judgment to recognize and avoid choices that could be detrimental to them;" that they "are more vulnerable or susceptible to . . . outside pressures" than adults, and so on. Describing no one child in particular, these observations restate what "any parent knows"—indeed, what any person knows—about children generally. . . .

Indeed, even where a "reasonable person" standard otherwise applies, the common law has reflected the reality that children are not adults. . . .

As this discussion establishes, "[o]ur history is replete with laws and judicial recognition" that children cannot be viewed simply as miniature adults. We see no justification for taking a different course here. So long as the child's age was known to the officer at the time of the interview, or would have been objectively apparent to any reasonable officer, including age as part of the custody analysis requires officers neither to consider circumstances "unknowable" to them, nor to "anticipat[e] the frailties or idiosyncrasies" of the particular suspect whom they question. The same "wide basis of community experience" that makes it possible, as an objective matter, "to determine what is to be expected" of children in other contexts, likewise makes it possible to know what to expect of children subjected to police questioning.

In other words, a child's age differs from other personal characteristics that, even when known to police, have no objectively discernible relationship to a reasonable person's understanding of his freedom of action. . . .

[W]e hold that so long as the child's age was known to the officer at the time of police questioning, or would have been objectively apparent to a reasonable officer, its inclusion in the custody analysis is consistent with the objective nature of that test. This is not to say that a child's age will be a determinative, or even a significant, factor in every case. It is, however, a reality that courts cannot simply ignore. . . .

The question remains whether J. D. B. was in custody when police interrogated him. We remand for the state courts to address that question, this time taking account of all of the relevant circumstances of the interrogation, including J. D. B.'s age at the time. The judgment of the North Carolina Supreme Court is reversed, and the case is remanded for proceedings not inconsistent with this opinion.

☐ *Justice ALITO, with whom THE CHIEF JUSTICE, Justice SCALIA, and Justice THOMAS join, dissenting.*

The Court's decision in this case may seem on first consideration to be modest and sensible, but in truth it is neither. It is fundamentally inconsistent with one of the main justifications for the *Miranda* rule: the perceived need for a clear rule that can be easily applied in all cases. And today's holding is not needed to protect the constitutional rights of minors who are questioned by the police.

Miranda's prophylactic regime places a high value on clarity and certainty. Dissatisfied with the highly fact-specific constitutional rule against the admission of involuntary confessions, the *Miranda* Court set down rigid standards that often require courts to ignore personal characteristics that may be highly relevant to a particular suspect's actual susceptibility to police pressure. This rigidity, however, has brought with it one of *Miranda's* principal strengths— "the ease and clarity of its application" by law enforcement officials and courts. A key contributor to this clarity, at least up until now, has been *Miranda's* objective reasonable-person test for determining custody.

Miranda's custody requirement is based on the proposition that the risk of unconstitutional coercion is heightened when a suspect is placed under formal arrest or is subjected to some functionally equivalent limitation on freedom of movement. When this custodial threshold is reached, *Miranda* warnings must precede police questioning. But in the interest of simplicity, the custody analysis considers only whether, under the circumstances, a hypothetical reasonable person would consider himself to be confined.

Many suspects, of course, will differ from this hypothetical reasonable person. Some, including those who have been hardened by past interrogations, may have no need for *Miranda* warnings at all. And for other suspects—those who are unusually sensitive to the pressures of police questioning—*Miranda* warnings may come too late to be of any use. That is a necessary consequence of *Miranda*'s rigid standards, but it does not mean that the constitutional rights of these especially sensitive suspects are left unprotected. A vulnerable defendant can still turn to the constitutional rule against actual coercion and contend that that his confession was extracted against his will.

Today's decision shifts the *Miranda* custody determination from a one-size-fits-all reasonable-person test into an inquiry that must account for at least one individualized characteristic—age—that is thought to correlate with susceptibility to coercive pressures. Age, however, is in no way the only personal characteristic that may correlate with pliability, and in future cases the Court will be forced to choose between two unpalatable alternatives. It may choose to limit today's decision by arbitrarily distinguishing a suspect's age from other personal characteristics—such as intelligence, education, occupation, or prior experience with law enforcement—that may also correlate with susceptibility to coercive pressures. Or, if the Court is unwilling to draw these arbitrary lines, it will be forced to effect a fundamental transformation of the *Miranda* custody test—from a clear, easily applied prophylactic rule into a highly fact-intensive standard resembling the voluntariness test that the *Miranda* Court found to be unsatisfactory.

For at least three reasons, there is no need to go down this road. First, many minors subjected to police interrogation are near the age of majority, and for these suspects the one-size-fits-all *Miranda* custody rule may not be a bad fit. Second, many of the difficulties in applying the *Miranda* custody rule to minors arise because of the unique circumstances present when the police conduct interrogations at school. The *Miranda* custody rule has always taken into account the setting in which questioning occurs, and accounting for the school setting in such cases will address many of these problems. Third, in cases like the one now before us, where the suspect is especially young, courts applying the constitutional voluntariness standard can take special care to ensure that incriminating statements were not obtained through coercion. . . .

No less than other facets of *Miranda*, the threshold requirement that the suspect be in "custody" is "designed to give clear guidance to the police." *Yarborough v. Alvarado*, 541 U.S. 652 (2004). Custody under *Miranda* attaches where there is a "formal arrest" or a "restraint on freedom of movement" akin to formal arrest. This standard is "objective" and turns on how a hypothetical "reasonable person in the position of the individual being questioned would gauge the breadth of his or her freedom of action."

Until today, the Court's cases applying this test have focused solely on the "objective circumstances of the interrogation," not the personal characteristics of the interrogated. Relevant factors have included such things as where the questioning occurred, how long it lasted, what was said, any physical restraints placed on the suspect's movement, and whether the suspect was allowed to leave when the questioning was through. The totality of these circumstances—the external circumstances, that is, of the interrogation itself—is what has mattered in this Court's cases. Personal characteristics of suspects have consistently been rejected or ignored as irrelevant under a one-size-fits-all reasonable-person standard. . . .

The Court's rationale for importing age into the custody standard is that minors tend to lack adults' "capacity to exercise mature judgment" and that failing to account for that "reality" will leave some minors unprotected under

Miranda in situations where they perceive themselves to be confined. I do not dispute that many suspects who are under 18 will be more susceptible to police pressure than the average adult. As the Court notes, our pre-*Miranda* cases were particularly attuned to this "reality" in applying the constitutional requirement of voluntariness in fact. Yet the *Miranda* custody standard has never accounted for the personal characteristics of these or any other individual defendants. . . .

The Court's decision greatly diminishes the clarity and administrability that have long been recognized as "principal advantages" of *Miranda*'s prophylactic requirements. But what is worse, the Court takes this step unnecessarily, as there are other, less disruptive tools available to ensure that minors are not coerced into confessing.

As an initial matter, the difficulties that the Court's standard introduces will likely yield little added protection for most juvenile defendants. Most juveniles who are subjected to police interrogation are teenagers nearing the age of majority. These defendants' reactions to police pressure are unlikely to be much different from the reaction of a typical 18-year-old in similar circumstances. A one-size-fits-all *Miranda* custody rule thus provides a roughly reasonable fit for these defendants. . . .

Finally, in cases like the one now before us, where the suspect is much younger than the typical juvenile defendant, courts should be instructed to take particular care to ensure that incriminating statements were not obtained involuntarily. The voluntariness inquiry is flexible and accommodating by nature, and the Court's precedents already make clear that "special care" must be exercised in applying the voluntariness test where the confession of a "mere child" is at issue. If *Miranda*'s rigid, one-size-fits-all standards fail to account for the unique needs of juveniles, the response should be to rigorously apply the constitutional rule against coercion to ensure that the rights of minors are protected. There is no need to run *Miranda* off the rails. . . .

I respectfully dissent.

9

THE RIGHT TO COUNSEL
AND OTHER PROCEDURAL
GUARANTEES

F | *The Right to Be Informed of Charges and to Confront Accusers*

The Court continues to confront litigation over its ruling in *Crawford v. Washington*, 541 U.S. 36 (2004). There, writing for a unanimous Court, Justice Scalia ostensibly laid down a bright-line rule that the prosecution may use statements of an absent witness against the accused at trial only if they were previously cross-examined by the defense counsel at a deposition or in a prior trial. But since *Crawford* the Court has carved out some exceptions, dealing for example with the use of child abuse victims' statements against defendants, in balancing the Sixth Amendment's guarantee of defendants' right to confront witnesses and the introduction of hearsay evidence at trial (see Vol. 2, Ch. 9).

In its 2010–2011 term the Court dealt with Sixth Amendment confrontation claims in two cases. In *Michigan v. Bryant*, 131 S.Ct. 1143 (2011), a majority of the Court held that a dying victim's statements identifying the assailant could be introduced at trial against the defendant. Richard Byrant, who had been shot in a parking lot, identified his assailant to police investigating the crime scene and died shortly afterward. His statements were introduced at trial but held by the state supreme court to violate the Sixth Amendment and to run afoul of the ruling in *Crawford*. But writing for a majority, Justice Sotomayor distinguished the application of *Crawford*'s ruling and the statements here as "nontestimonial" because they were made to police at the time they were responding to "an on-going emergency" and there was a "potential threat to the responding police and the public at large." By contrast, statements to police that amount to "testimony" about the accused are not allowed to be used at trial. Dissenting Justice Scalia, the author of the decision in *Crawford*, sharply rejected the majority's distinction between nontestimonial and testimonial in limiting the holding in *Crawford*. Justice Ginsburg also dissented, on separate grounds.

In a second decision, in *Bullcoming v. New Mexico*, 131 S.Ct. 2705 (2011), the Court confronted the issue of whether crime lab reports may be introduced as evidence against the defendant even though the author of the report is unavailable to testify against the defendant. Donald Bullcoming struck a car at a stop sign and was later alleged to have been driving under the influence of alcohol. After he left the crime scene, he allegedly went for drinks with friends, subsequently was located again by police, and failed a gas chromatograph test for blood alcohol content. The analyst who signed the forensic report was unavailable to testify at trial, and prosecutors called another analyst from the lab to testify. At issue, thus, was if a lab machine provides the incriminating evidence against the accused, does it matter which lab analyst testifies about the lab results and confronts the accused? Writing for a bare majority, Justice Ginsburg held that the Confrontation Clause does not permit the prosecution to introduce a forensic report, containing a testimonial certification, and call an analyst who did not conduct, observe, or certify the test reported. The accused right is to confront the analyst who made the certification and, if unavailable at trial, the accused must have an opportunity during a pretrial hearing to cross-examine that particular scientist.

10

CRUEL AND UNUSUAL PUNISHMENT

I n a controversial ruling in *Brown v. Plata*, 131 S.Ct. 1910 (2011), a bare majority of the Court affirmed a three-judge-court-issued injunction for the release of approximately 40,000 inmates in California's prison system due to overcrowding that created conditions of cruel and unusual punishment in violation of the Eighth Amendment. The system was designed to house about 80,000 but at various times held between 140,000 and more than 160,000 prisoners; and the lower court ordered a reduction of the prison population to 100,000. In affirming the lower court, the majority emphasized that, "As many as 200 prisoners may live in a gymnasium, monitored by as few as two or three correctional officers . . . [and that as] many as 54 prisoners may share a single toilet, as well as that about one prisoner per week commits suicide." Writing for the Court, Justice Kennedy acknowledged that, "The release of prisoners in large numbers—assuming the state finds no other way to comply with the order—is a matter of un-doubted, grave concern." "Yet," he stressed, "so too is the contin-uing injury and harm resulting from these serious constitutional violations." "A prison that deprives prisoners of basic sustenance, including adequate medical care, is incompatible with the concept of human dignity and has no place in civilized society." In com-plying with the court's order, Justice Kennedy underscored that the state could achieve the reduction by a variety of means, including releasing the least dangerous convicts, transferring inmates to other prisons, and building more prisons. Justices Ginsburg, Breyer, Sotomayor, and Kagan joined his opinion.

By contrast, dissenting Justice Scalia, joined by Justice Thomas, blasted the majority for affirming "perhaps the most radical injunction issued by a court in our nation's history." They emphasized that courts exceed their authority and are ill equipped to bring about such major changes through "structural injunctions" and "institutional-reform litigation." In a separate dissent Justice Alito, joined by Chief Justice Roberts, lamented the inevitable impact on public safety: "I fear that today's decision, like prior prisoner-release orders, will lead to a grim roster of victims. I hope that I am wrong. In a few years, we will see."

INDEX OF CASES

Cases printed in boldface are excerpted on the page(s) printed in boldface.

Other Books by David M. O'Brien

Storm Center:
The Supreme Court in American Politics
9th ed.

Constitutional Law and Politics:
Vol. 1. *Struggles for Power and Governmental Accountability*
Vol. 2. *Civil Rights and Civil Liberties*
8th ed.

Congress Shall Make No Law: The First Amendment,
Unprotected Expression, and the U.S. Supreme Court

Animal Sacrifice and Religious Freedom:
Church of Lukumi Babalu Aye v. City of Hialeah

To Dream of Dreams:
Religious Freedom and Constitutional Politics in Postwar Japan

Judicial Roulette

What Process Is Due?
Courts and Science-Policy Disputes

The Public's Right to Know:
The Supreme Court and the First Amendment

Privacy, Law, and Public Policy

Judges on Judging: Views from the Bench
3rd ed. (editor)

The Lanahan Readings on Civil Rights and Civil Liberties
3rd ed. (editor)

Abortion and American Politics
(co-author)

Judicial Independence in the Age of Democracy:
Critical Perspectives from Around the World
(co-editor)

The Politics of Technology Assessment:
Institutions, Processes, and Policy Disputes
(co-editor)

Views from the Bench:
The Judiciary and Constitutional Politics
(co-editor)

The Politics of American Government
3rd ed. (co-author)

Government by the People
22nd ed. (co-author)

Courts and Judicial Policymaking
(co-author)